THE 7 CONTINENTS

AUSTRALIA & OCEANIA

CONTENTS

Downloadable Maps

Ten maps used in this book are available for download on our Web site, as well as two color maps: one projection map of the world and one political map of Australia and Oceania.

How to Download:

1. Go to www.evan-moor.com/resources.

2. Enter your e-mail address and the resource code for this product—EMC3733.

3. You will receive an e-mail with a link to the downloadable maps.

What's in This Book

▶ **5 sections** of reproducible information and activity pages centered on five main topics: Australia and Oceania in the World, Political Divisions, Physical Features, Valuable Resources, and Culture.

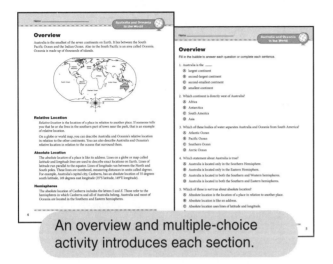

An overview and multiple-choice activity introduces each section.

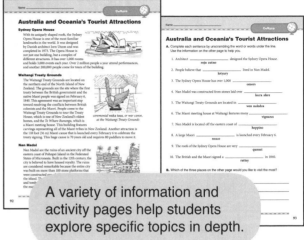

A variety of information and activity pages help students explore specific topics in depth.

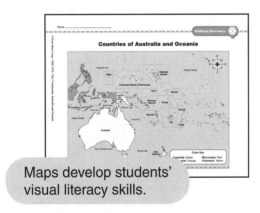

Maps develop students' visual literacy skills.

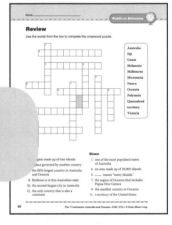

A crossword puzzle at the end of each section provides a fun review activity.

▶ **1 section** of assessment activities

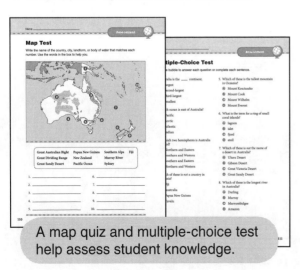

A map quiz and multiple-choice test help assess student knowledge.

▶ **1 section** of open-ended note takers

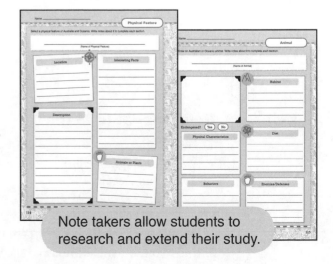

Note takers allow students to research and extend their study.

Australia and Oceania in the World

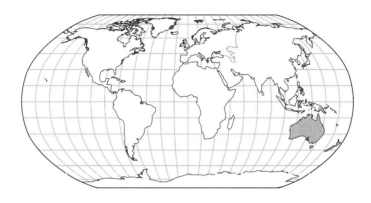

This section introduces students to the location of Australia and Oceania in the world. Students learn about the difference between relative and absolute location, as well as the hemispheres in which Australia and Oceania lie. Students also practice using lines of latitude and longitude to find places on a map.

Each skill in this section is based on the following National Geography Standards:

Essential Element 1: The World in Spatial Terms

Standard 1: How to use maps and other geographic representations, tools, and technologies to acquire, process, and report information from a spatial perspective

CONTENTS

Overview

Australia is the smallest of the seven continents on Earth. It lies between the South Pacific Ocean and the Indian Ocean. Also in the South Pacific is an area called Oceania. Oceania is made up of thousands of islands.

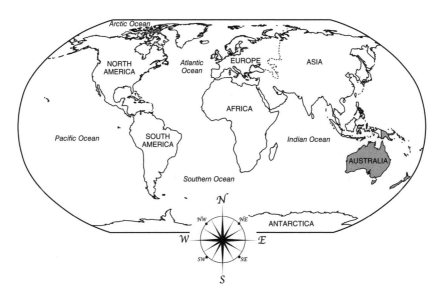

Relative Location

Relative location is the location of a place in relation to another place. If someone tells you that he or she lives in the southern part of town near the park, that is an example of relative location.

On a globe or world map, you can describe Australia and Oceania's relative location in relation to the other continents. You can also describe Australia and Oceania's relative location in relation to the oceans that surround them.

Absolute Location

The *absolute location* of a place is like its address. Lines on a globe or map called *latitude* and *longitude lines* are used to describe exact locations on Earth. Lines of latitude run parallel to the equator. Lines of longitude run between the North and South poles. These lines are numbered, measuring distances in units called *degrees*. For example, Australia's capital city, Canberra, has an absolute location of 35 degrees south latitude, 149 degrees east longitude (35°S latitude, 149°E longitude).

Hemispheres

The absolute location of Canberra includes the letters *S* and *E*. Those refer to the hemispheres in which Canberra and all of Australia belong. Australia and most of Oceania are located in the Southern and Eastern hemispheres.

Overview

Fill in the bubble to answer each question or complete each sentence.

1. Australia is the _____.

   Ⓐ largest continent

   Ⓑ second-largest continent

   Ⓒ second-smallest continent

   Ⓓ smallest continent

2. Which continent is directly west of Australia?

   Ⓐ Africa

   Ⓑ Antarctica

   Ⓒ South America

   Ⓓ Asia

3. Which of these bodies of water separates Australia and Oceania from South America?

   Ⓐ Atlantic Ocean

   Ⓑ Pacific Ocean

   Ⓒ Southern Ocean

   Ⓓ Arctic Ocean

4. Which statement about Australia is true?

   Ⓐ Australia is located only in the Southern Hemisphere.

   Ⓑ Australia is located only in the Eastern Hemisphere.

   Ⓒ Australia is located in both the Southern and Western hemispheres.

   Ⓓ Australia is located in both the Southern and Eastern hemispheres.

5. Which of these is *not* true about absolute location?

   Ⓐ Absolute location is the location of a place in relation to another place.

   Ⓑ Absolute location is like an address.

   Ⓒ Absolute location uses lines of latitude and longitude.

   Ⓓ Absolute location is measured in degrees.

Name _____

Australia and Oceania's Relative Location

Relative location is the position of a place in relation to another place. How would you describe where Australia and Oceania are located in the world using relative location?

Look at the world map on the other page. One way to describe where Australia and Oceania are located is to name the other continents that border them. For example, Australia is southeast of Asia and Oceania is east of Australia.

Another way to describe the relative location of Australia and Oceania is to name the oceans that surround the continent and islands. For example, the Indian Ocean is west of Australia. And the islands of Oceania are actually in the Pacific Ocean.

A. Use the map on the other page to complete the paragraph about the relative location of Australia and Oceania.

Australia is the smallest continent in the world. It is located east of the continent

of _____ and northeast of _____.

Australia is also located to the _____ of Oceania. The

_____ Ocean is to the west of Australia. The Pacific Ocean

is to the _____ of the small continent. Finally, the islands

of _____ are all located in the _____

Ocean.

B. Follow the directions to color the map on the other page.

1. Color the continent directly west of Australia orange.

2. Color the continent south of Australia gray.

3. Use blue to circle the name of the ocean in which Oceania is located.

4. Draw a panda on the continent northwest of Australia.

Australia and Oceania's Relative Location

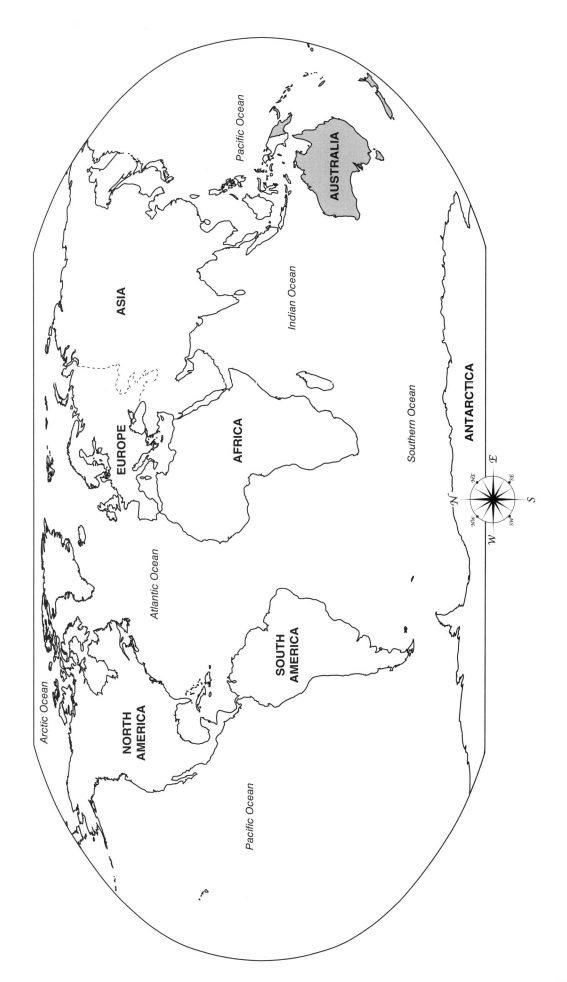

Australia and Oceania's Hemispheres

On a globe, Earth is divided into four hemispheres by a horizontal line called the *equator* and by vertical lines that run from the North Pole to the South Pole. The hemispheres are the Northern, Southern, Western, and Eastern. Australia and most of the islands that make up Oceania are part of the Southern Hemisphere because they are south of the equator. Australia and many islands of Oceania are also located in the Eastern Hemisphere.

Northern and Southern Hemispheres

A globe shows a horizontal imaginary line that runs around the center of Earth. This line is called the *equator*. The equator divides Earth into the Northern and Southern hemispheres.

Since Australia and most of Oceania are south of the equator, they are mostly in the Southern Hemisphere.

Eastern and Western Hemispheres

A globe also shows imaginary vertical lines that run from the North Pole to the South Pole, the southernmost point on Earth. One of these vertical lines is called the *prime meridian*. This line, along with its twin line on the opposite side of the globe, create the Western and Eastern hemispheres.

Since Australia and parts of Oceania are east of the prime meridian, they are in the Eastern Hemisphere.

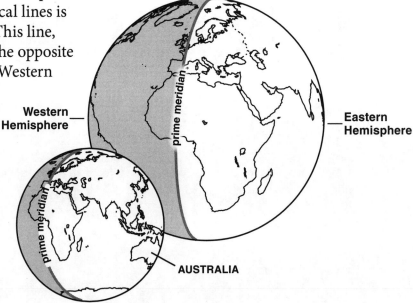

The 7 Continents: Australia and Oceania • EMC 3733 • © Evan-Moor Corp.

Australia and Oceania's Hemispheres

A. Write the letter of the definition that matches each term. Use the information on the other page to help you.

_____ 1. Australia

_____ 2. continent

_____ 3. globe

_____ 4. equator

_____ 5. Eastern Hemisphere

_____ 6. hemisphere

_____ 7. South Pole

_____ 8. Southern Hemisphere

_____ 9. prime meridian

a. an imaginary line that runs from the North Pole to the South Pole

b. half of Earth

c. the continent that is in both the Southern and Eastern hemispheres

d. the hemisphere that is east of the prime meridian

e. an imaginary line that divides Earth into the Northern and Southern hemispheres

f. any of the seven large landmasses of Earth

g. the southernmost point on Earth

h. a round model of Earth

i. the hemisphere that is south of the equator

B. Label the parts of the globe. Use the letters next to the terms in the box.

A. Eastern
   Hemisphere

B. Southern
   Hemisphere

C. Australia

D. equator

E. prime
   meridian

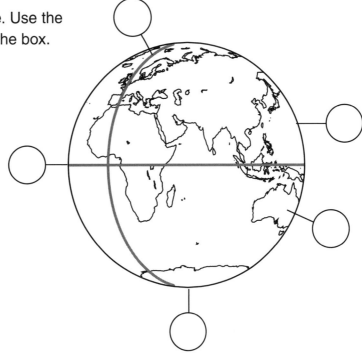

Name _____

Australia and Oceania's Absolute Location

Many globes contain lines that make it easier to find specific places on Earth. Lines of latitude measure the distance north and south of the equator. Lines of longitude measure the distance east and west of the prime meridian. You can use lines of latitude and longitude to find the absolute location of Australia and Oceania on a globe.

Latitude

The equator is found at the absolute location of 0° (zero degrees) latitude. Other lines of latitude run parallel to the equator, and are labeled with an *N* or *S*, depending on whether they are north or south of the equator. Latitude lines are also called *parallels*.

On the picture of the globe, notice the lines of latitude. Look for the continent of Australia. Since the continent is south of the equator, all the latitude lines used to find the absolute location of places within Australia are labeled in *degrees south*, or °S.

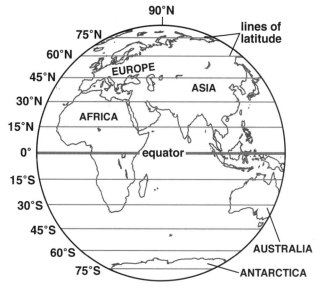

Lines of Latitude (Parallels)

Longitude

The prime meridian runs from the North Pole to the South Pole at 0° (zero degrees) longitude. Other lines of longitude run north and south, too, and are labeled with an *E* or *W*, depending on whether they are east or west of the prime meridian. Longitude lines are also called *meridians*.

On the picture of the globe, notice the lines of longitude. Look for the continent of Australia. Since the continent is east of the prime meridian, all the longitude lines used to find the absolute location of places within Australia are labeled in *degrees east*, or °E.

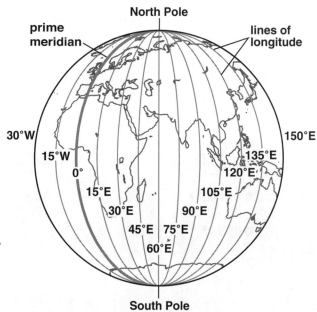

Lines of Longitude (Meridians)

Name _____

Australia and Oceania's Absolute Location

To find the absolute location of a place, read the latitude line first and then read the longitude line. For example, the latitude 40°S runs through southern New Zealand, a country in Oceania. The longitude 170°E also runs through southern New Zealand. So the absolute location of southern New Zealand is 40°S latitude, 170°E longitude.

A. Circle the correct answer to each question. Use the pictures of the globes and information on the other page to help you.

1. Which line is at 0 degrees latitude?   **equator**   **prime meridian**

2. Which line runs north and south?   **equator**   **prime meridian**

3. In which direction is Australia from the equator?   **north**   **south**

4. Which line of longitude runs through Australia?   **120°E**   **120°W**

5. Which line of latitude runs through Australia?   **30°S**   **30°N**

6. Which lines run parallel to the equator?   **latitude lines**   **longitude lines**

7. How many degrees are between each line of latitude and longitude on the globe pictures?   **10 degrees**   **15 degrees**

8. What is another name for lines of latitude?   **meridians**   **parallels**

9. Which line of latitude is closer to the equator?   **15°S**   **30°S**

10. Which line of longitude is farther east?   **150°E**   **120°E**

B. Using the information on the other page, explain why most places in Australia and Oceania have absolute locations that are labeled in degrees south and east.

_____

_____

Using a Projection Map

How do you draw a picture of a round object, such as Earth, on a flat piece of paper? In order to show all of Earth's continents and oceans in one view, mapmakers use a system called *projection*. Mapping the round Earth on a flat surface causes some areas to look bigger than they really are. For example, land near the poles gets stretched out when flattened. That's why Greenland and Antarctica look so big on some maps.

A projection map of the world shows all the lines of latitude and longitude on Earth. Study the projection map on the other page. Notice the lines of latitude and longitude. You can use these lines to find the absolute location of a specific place in Australia and Oceania. For example, the label *Australia* is located at 25°S latitude, 135°E longitude.

Read each statement. Circle **yes** if it is true or **no** if it is false. Use the map on the other page to help you.

1. Australia is located on the prime meridian.   **Yes**   **No**

2. Australia is located south of the equator.   **Yes**   **No**

3. The southern part of Australia is between the latitudes
   of 30°S and 45°S.   **Yes**   **No**

4. Australia is the only continent east of the prime meridian.   **Yes**   **No**

5. Australia shares some of the same south latitude lines
   with Africa.   **Yes**   **No**

6. Australia shares some of the same east longitude lines with Asia. **Yes**   **No**

7. The longitude line 120°E runs through Australia and Europe.   **Yes**   **No**

8. The latitude line 30°S runs through Australia, Africa, and
   South America.   **Yes**   **No**

9. The latitude line 15°S runs through Australia and three
   different oceans.   **Yes**   **No**

10. The longitude line 120°E runs through western Australia.   **Yes**   **No**

The 7 Continents: Australia and Oceania • EMC 3733 • © Evan-Moor Corp.

Name _____

Using a Projection Map

NORTH
AMERICA

SOUTH
AMERICA

EUROPE

ASIA

AFRICA

AUSTRALIA

ANTARCTICA

Arctic Ocean

Pacific Ocean

Atlantic Ocean

Pacific Ocean

Indian Ocean

Southern Ocean

prime meridian

equator

180° 150°W 120°W 90°W 60°W 30°W 0° 30°E 60°E 90°E 120°E 150°E 180°

75°N
60°N
45°N
30°N
15°N
0°
15°S
30°S
45°S
60°S
75°S
90°S

N NE
NW
W E
SW SE
S

Review

Use words from the box to complete the crossword puzzle.

absolute

Africa

equator

hemispheres

islands

Pacific

projection

smallest

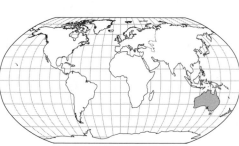

Across

1. Australia is part of the Southern and Eastern _____.

3. If you go west of Australia you will find the continent of _____.

6. The _____ is the imaginary line that divides the Northern and Southern hemispheres.

7. The Indian and _____ oceans border Australia.

Down

2. Australia is the _____ continent in the world.

3. _____ location uses lines of latitude and longitude to describe where a place is located.

4. Oceania is made up of thousands of _____.

5. A _____ map shows the round Earth on a flat surface.

Political Divisions of Australia and Oceania

This section introduces students to the four regions and 14 countries of Australia and Oceania. Students study information about the largest and smallest countries in size and population. They also learn about the dependent territories in Oceania, as well as the capital cities of independent nations.

Each skill in this section is based on the following National Geography Standards:

Essential Element 2: Places and Regions

Standard 5: People create regions to interpret Earth's complexity

Essential Element 4: Human Systems

Standard 9: The characteristics, distribution, and migration of human populations on Earth's surface

CONTENTS

Overview

Australia is the smallest of the seven continents. It is the only country in the world that is also a continent. Many geographers group Australia with a region called Oceania, which is made up of about 30,000 small islands.

- Australia and Oceania cover 3,278,062 square miles (8,490,180 square km).

- Australia and Oceania have nearly 36 million people combined.

The Four Regions

The country of Australia is considered a region within the continental grouping of Australia and Oceania. The remaining 13 countries of Oceania are divided into three regions—Melanesia, Micronesia, and Polynesia.

Region	Number of Countries	Fast Facts
Australia	1	the largest country in Australia/Oceania
Melanesia	4	includes the largest country in Oceania—Papua New Guinea
Micronesia	5	includes 4 of the 5 smallest countries in Oceania
Polynesia	4	includes the second-largest country in Oceania—New Zealand

Where People Live

The most populated country in the Australia/Oceania region is Australia. Over 21 million people live there. Nine out of every 10 people in Australia live in cities or towns near the southeastern coast. The largest city in Australia is Sydney, with over 4 million people. There are only four other Australian cities that have more than 1 million people. They are Melbourne, Brisbane, Perth, and Adelaide. Most of the interior of Australia, which is often called the Outback, is barren, dry, and sparsely populated.

Other than Papua New Guinea and New Zealand, none of the other countries in Oceania have more than 1 million people. Most of the people who live on these islands live in small farming or fishing villages. Large cities are rare.

Overview

Fill in the bubble to complete each sentence.

1. Australia is _____.

   Ⓐ a continent that is made up of about 30,000 islands

   Ⓑ the largest continent

   Ⓒ the only country that is also a continent

   Ⓓ located in the region of Polynesia

2. There are _____ countries in Australia and Oceania combined.

   Ⓐ 4

   Ⓑ 5

   Ⓒ 14

   Ⓓ 23

3. Most Australians live in _____.

   Ⓐ cities or towns near the coast

   Ⓑ the Outback

   Ⓒ Sydney

   Ⓓ small farming and fishing villages

4. The largest country in Oceania is _____.

   Ⓐ Micronesia

   Ⓑ Papua New Guinea

   Ⓒ New Zealand

   Ⓓ Australia

5. New Zealand has a population of _____.

   Ⓐ about 21 million

   Ⓑ about 400,000

   Ⓒ less than 1 million

   Ⓓ more than 1 million

Population of Australia and Oceania

Between 1950 and 2010, the world population nearly tripled. The combined population of Australia and Oceania is growing at about the same rate. In 1950, there were fewer than 15 million people in Australia and Oceania. By 2010, the number had grown to over 35 million. And by 2050, the total population of Australia and Oceania is expected to be over 50 million.

Population of Australia and Oceania: 1950–2050

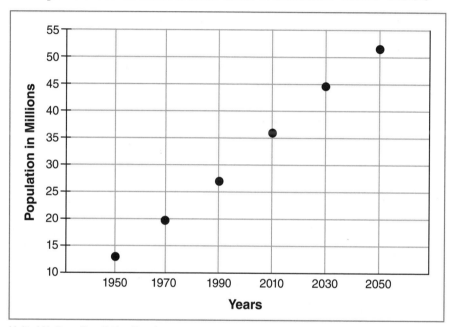

United Nations Population Database

A. Draw a line that connects the dots to complete the line graph above.

B. Write two questions that can be answered using the information on the graph. Then write the answers.

1. _____

_____

2. _____

_____

Population of Australia and Oceania

c. Circle the answer that completes each sentence. Use the graph and information on the other page to help you.

1. The population of the world has nearly ____ since 1950.

   doubled   **tripled**   **quadrupled**

2. Compared to the world population, the population of Australia and Oceania is growing ____.

   faster   **slower**   **at about the same rate**

3. In 1950, there were about ____ million people living in Australia and Oceania.

   13   **19**   **30**

4. By 1970, there were nearly ____ million more people in Australia and Oceania than there were in 1950.

   5   **7**   **9**

5. In 2010, there were over ____ million people in Australia and Oceania.

   44   **35**   **51**

6. By 2030, there will be about ____ million people in Australia and Oceania.

   51   **35**   **45**

7. There will be nearly ____ times as many people living in Australia and Oceania in 2050 as there were in 1950.

   two   **three**   **four**

8. There were about 27 million people living in Australia and Oceania in ____.

   1950   **1990**   **2010**

Countries of Australia and Oceania

Together, the continent of Australia and the nearby islands of Oceania include 14 independent nations, as well as many dependent territories. The country of Australia is by far the largest independent nation in size and population. The tiny island nation of Nauru, located northeast of Australia, is the smallest.

Several countries in Oceania, such as the Marshall Islands, Solomon Islands, and the Federated States of Micronesia, are made up of groups of islands called *archipelagos*. Many of these island countries are smaller in size and population than some U.S. cities!

A. Look at the chart of the four regions of Australia and Oceania below. Then find the countries on the map on the other page. Use the color key on the map to circle the name of each country in the color of its region.

Region	Countries
Australia	Australia
Melanesia	Fiji Papua New Guinea Solomon Islands Vanuatu
Micronesia	Kiribati Marshall Islands Federated States of Micronesia Nauru Palau
Polynesia	New Zealand Samoa Tonga Tuvalu

B. Answer the questions using the information above.

1. Which region has the most countries? _____

2. Which region has the fewest countries? _____

3. Name three countries that are archipelagos.

_____

Countries of Australia and Oceania

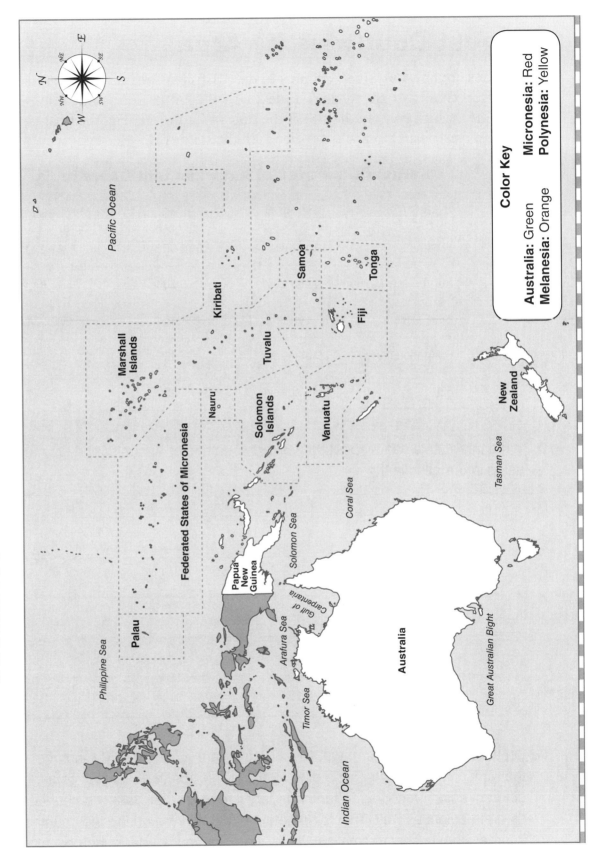

Color Key

Australia: Green   Micronesia: Red
Melanesia: Orange   Polynesia: Yellow

New Zealand

Australia

Papua New Guinea

Palau

Federated States of Micronesia

Marshall Islands

Nauru

Kiribati

Tuvalu

Samoa

Tonga

Fiji

Solomon Islands

Vanuatu

Pacific Ocean

Philippine Sea

Timor Sea

Arafura Sea

Gulf of Carpentaria

Solomon Sea

Coral Sea

Tasman Sea

Indian Ocean

Great Australian Bight

Largest Countries by Area

Australia is not only the largest country in the Australia/Oceania region, but it is also the sixth-largest country in the world. The next-largest country in Australia/Oceania is Papua New Guinea, which is about the size of the state of California. Fiji, the fifth-largest country in Australia/Oceania, is smaller than the state of New Jersey.

Largest Countries of Australia and Oceania

	Country	Region	Square Miles	Square Kilometers
1	Australia	Australia	2,988,902	7,741,220
2	Papua New Guinea	Melanesia	178,704	462,840
3	New Zealand	Polynesia	104,454	270,534
4	Solomon Islands	Melanesia	11,157	28,896
5	Fiji	Melanesia	7,056	18,274

A. Write three statements about the largest countries of Australia and Oceania, using information in the chart.

1. _____

_____

2. _____

_____

3. _____

_____

B. On the map on the other page, five countries are numbered. The numbers indicate the rank of each country according to size. Color the three largest countries a different color. Trace the dotted boundary line around the last two countries in different colors as well. Then complete the map key by writing the country names in order from largest to smallest. Write the color you used for each country.

Largest Countries by Area

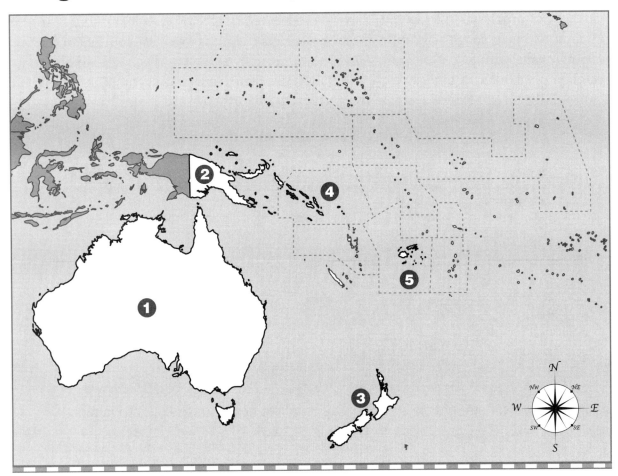

MAP KEY

The Five Largest Countries   Color

1. _____   _____

2. _____   _____

3. _____   _____

4. _____   _____

5. _____   _____

Smallest Countries by Area

Some of the smallest countries in the world are located in Oceania. At just 8 square miles (21 square km) in area, the island nation of Nauru is the third-smallest country in the world. Tuvalu, with just 10 square miles (26 square km), is the world's fourth-smallest country. The land area of all five of the smallest countries in Oceania combined is less than half the size of Rhode Island—the smallest state in the United States!

Smallest Countries of Oceania

Country	Region	Square Miles	Square Kilometers
Federated States of Micronesia	Micronesia	271	702
Marshall Islands	Micronesia	70	181
Nauru	Micronesia	8	21
Palau	Micronesia	177	459
Tuvalu	Polynesia	10	26

A. Write three statements about Oceania's smallest countries, using information in the chart.

1. _____

_____

2. _____

_____

3. _____

_____

B. On the map on the other page, five groups of islands that form countries are numbered. The numbers indicate the rank of each island nation according to size. Trace the dotted boundary line around each island country in a different color. Then complete the map key by writing the country names in order from smallest to largest. Write the color you used for each country.

Smallest Countries by Area

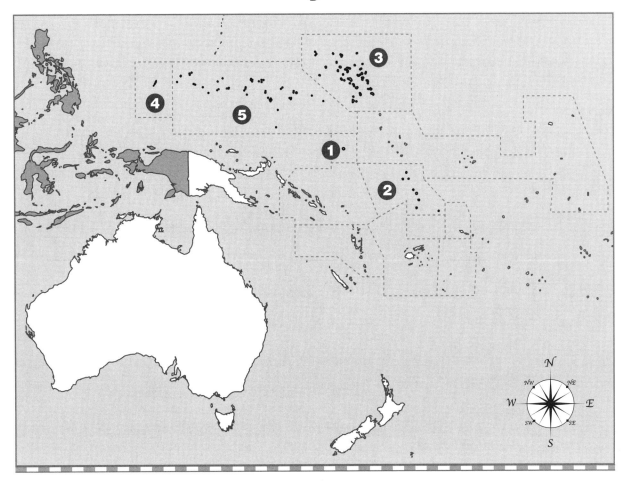

MAP KEY

The Five Smallest Countries   **Color**

1. _____   _____

2. _____   _____

3. _____   _____

4. _____   _____

5. _____   _____

Largest Countries by Population

Nearly two-thirds of the people in Australia and Oceania live in the country of Australia. The population of Oceania is scattered among the many islands that make up this region of the world. The largest populations of Oceania are on the two largest islands in size—Papua New Guinea and New Zealand.

A. Write the letter of the clue that describes each country. Use the chart on the other page to help you.

_____ 1. Australia

_____ 2. Fiji

_____ 3. Kiribati

_____ 4. Federated States of Micronesia

_____ 5. New Zealand

_____ 6. Papua New Guinea

_____ 7. Samoa

_____ 8. Solomon Islands

_____ 9. Tonga

_____ 10. Vanuatu

a. the eighth most populated country

b. has a population of just over half a million

c. has a population smaller than Kiribati

d. the most populated country

e. has a population of 218,519

f. the fourth most populated country

g. has just over 6 million people

h. the sixth most populated country

i. has a little more than 4 million people

j. has a population of 112,850

B. Use the chart on the other page to answer the questions.

1. How many countries in Australia and Oceania have populations over 1 million?   _____

2. The population of Australia is about how many times larger than the population of New Zealand?   _____

3. Which two countries are the closest in population?

_____

Largest Countries by Population

Countries with Populations
of More Than 100,000

	Country	Region	Population
1	Australia	Australia	21,262,641
2	Papua New Guinea	Melanesia	6,057,263
3	New Zealand	Polynesia	4,213,418
4	Fiji	Melanesia	944,720
5	Solomon Islands	Melanesia	595,613
6	Samoa	Polynesia	219,998
7	Vanuatu	Melanesia	218,519
8	Tonga	Polynesia	120,898
9	Kiribati	Micronesia	112,850
10	Federated States of Micronesia	Micronesia	107,434

c. Write three statements about the most populated countries of Australia and Oceania. Use the chart above to help you.

1. _____

_____

2. _____

_____

3. _____

_____

Dependent Territories

In addition to the 14 countries that make up Australia and Oceania, there are also 13 dependent territories in the region. Rather than being independent countries, these territories are governed by another country. Three of the countries that hold territories in Oceania—France, the United Kingdom, and the United States—are located far away from the territories in distant parts of the world.

Some of the territories are very small. The smallest, Midway Island, is just 2 square miles (5.2 square km) in area. Only about 40 people live on Midway Island. Wake Island and Tokelau are also only a few square miles in area. The largest territory is New Caledonia, which is over 7,000 square miles (18,500 square km) in size. The territory with the largest population is French Polynesia, with about 291,000 people.

Governing Country	Dependent Territory	Region	Area
Australia	Norfolk Island	Melanesia	14 square miles (35 square km)
France	French Polynesia	Polynesia	1,544 square miles (4,000 square km)
	New Caledonia	Melanesia	7,172 square miles (18,575 square km)
	Wallis and Futuna Islands	Polynesia	102 square miles (264 square km)
New Zealand	Cook Islands	Polynesia	91 square miles (236 square km)
	Niue Island	Polynesia	100 square miles (260 square km)
	Tokelau	Polynesia	5 square miles (12 square km)
United Kingdom	Pitcairn Islands Group	Polynesia	18 square miles (47 square km)
United States	American Samoa	Polynesia	77 square miles (199 square km)
	Guam	Micronesia	212 square miles (549 square km)
	Midway Island	Polynesia	2 square miles (5 square km)
	Northern Mariana Islands	Micronesia	179 square miles (464 square km)
	Wake Island	Micronesia	3 square miles (8 square km)

The 7 Continents: Australia and Oceania • EMC 3733 • © Evan-Moor Corp.

Dependent Territories

A. Circle the correct answer. Use the information on the other page to help you.

1. This is the smallest dependent territory.	**Midway Island**	**Wake Island**
2. This is a territory of New Zealand.	**Cook Islands**	**New Caledonia**
3. This territory is in Melanesia.	**Guam**	**New Caledonia**
4. This is the UK's only territory.	**Pitcairn Islands Group**	**Wallis and Futuna Islands**
5. American Samoa covers 199 square ____.	**miles**	**kilometers**
6. The second-smallest dependent territory is ____.	**Wake Island**	**Tokelau**
7. This is a dependent territory of the United States.	**Guam**	**Niue Island**
8. The Northern Mariana Islands are a territory of the ____.	**United Kingdom**	**United States**
9. This is the population of French Polynesia.	**291,000**	**18,500**

B. Use the information on the other page to answer the questions.

1. How many dependent territories are in Micronesia? _____

2. How many dependent territories are less than 100 square miles in size? _____

3. Which territory belongs to Australia? _____

4. Which region contains the most territories? _____

5. Which three dependent territories belong to New Zealand?

_____

Australia

Australia is often referred to as "the land down under" because it is located completely in the Southern Hemisphere. Australia is divided into six states and two mainland territories. The territories are similar to states but have a slightly different form of government. The states are New South Wales, Queensland, South Australia, Tasmania (an island off the southern coast), Victoria, and Western Australia. The two territories are the Australian Capital Territory, which is located within the state of New South Wales, and Northern Territory.

New South Wales and Victoria are the most populated states. Many people in these states live in big cities near the coast. Sydney, the largest city in Australia, is in New South Wales, and Melbourne, the second-largest city, is in Victoria. Other large cities include Brisbane, Queensland; Perth, Western Australia; and Adelaide, South Australia.

A. Read each statement. Circle **yes** if it is true or **no** if it is false. Use the information above and the map on the other page to help you.

1. The Northern Territory is a state in Australia.   **Yes**   **No**

2. Queensland is east of New South Wales.   **Yes**   **No**

3. Sydney is the largest city in Australia.   **Yes**   **No**

4. Victoria is an island off the southern coast of Australia.   **Yes**   **No**

5. Australia is located entirely north of the equator.   **Yes**   **No**

6. There are six states in Australia.   **Yes**   **No**

7. Perth is located in the state of Western Australia.   **Yes**   **No**

8. Most people in Australia live in big cities far from the coast.   **Yes**   **No**

9. Tasmania is located south of Victoria.   **Yes**   **No**

10. Brisbane is located on the east coast of Australia.   **Yes**   **No**

B. On the map on the other page, color each of the six states and two mainland territories of Australia a different color. Then write a caption below the map.

Australia

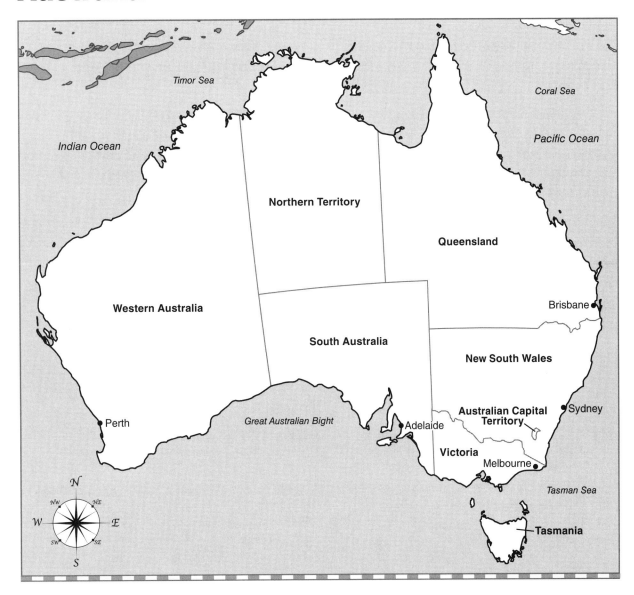

Melanesia

The region of Melanesia consists of a group of islands off the northeastern coast of Australia. The largest country in the region is Papua New Guinea, which is located on the eastern half of the island of New Guinea. The western half of the island, Papua, belongs to the country of Indonesia in Asia.

To the east of Papua New Guinea lie the Solomon Islands, which contain 10 large islands and many smaller ones. The nation of Vanuatu is southeast of the Solomon Islands. Vanuatu is made up of 82 small islands. On the far eastern side of Melanesia lies the country of Fiji. Although there are more than 330 islands in Fiji, most of the population lives on the two main islands of Viti Levu and Vanua Levu.

Melanesia also includes two dependent territories, which are both located in the southern part of the region. The French territory of New Caledonia is located southwest of Vanuatu. The territory of Norfolk Island, which belongs to Australia, is south of New Caledonia.

A. Fill in the blanks to answer each question. Use the information above and the map on the other page to help you.

1. Which of the countries in Melanesia is farthest west? _____

2. Which country is made up of 82 small islands? _____

3. Which country in Melanesia is farthest east? _____

4. Which country is north of Vanuatu and east of Papua New Guinea? _____

5. Which territory is south of New Caledonia? _____

6. What are the names of the two main islands in Fiji?

_____

B. On the map on the other page, circle the names of the four countries of Melanesia in green. Then circle the names of the two territories in red. Write which countries the territories belong to underneath their names.

Name _____

Melanesia

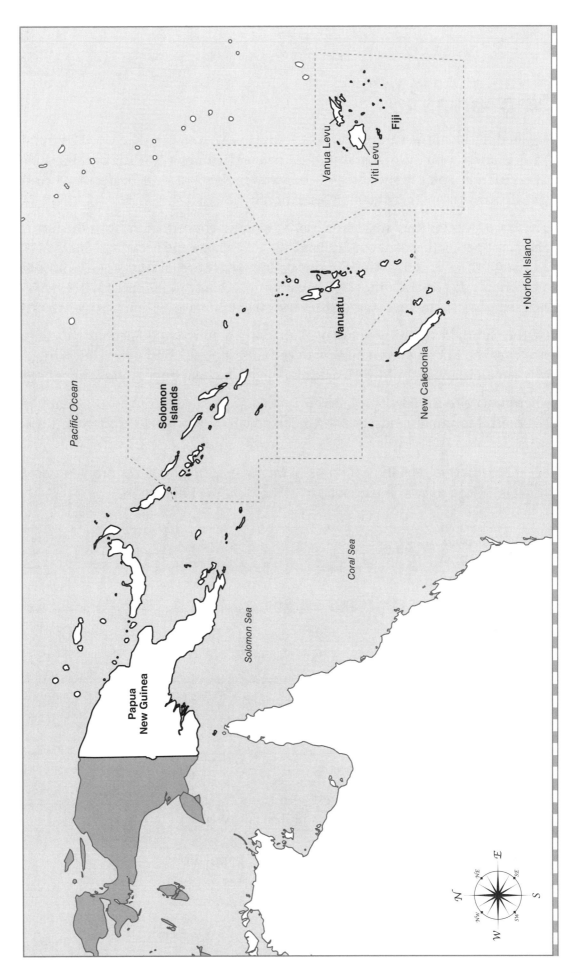

Pacific Ocean

Vanua Levu

Viti Levu

Fiji

Vanuatu

New Caledonia

Norfolk Island

Solomon Islands

Coral Sea

Solomon Sea

Papua New Guinea

Micronesia

Located in the northernmost part of Oceania is Micronesia. The word *Micronesia* means "tiny islands," and the region is well-named—Micronesia consists of thousands of very small islands. Some of the smallest countries in the world are located in Micronesia, spread across more than 4,000 miles of ocean.

There are five countries in Micronesia. The island country of Palau is the farthest west and has a population of about 21,000. East of Palau are the Federated States of Micronesia. Although there are 607 islands in this country, they are all very small, with a total land area of only 271 square miles (702 square km). About 107,000 people live there. The Marshall Islands to the east are also very small and have a population of about 65,000.

Farther south lies the tiny island of Nauru, where only 14,000 people live. But to its east stretches the Micronesia country with the largest population—Kiribati. Kiribati consists of 33 small islands, 21 of which are inhabited. The total population is about 113,000.

Micronesia also includes three territories that are located in the north: Guam, the Northern Mariana Islands, and Wake Island, all of which belong to the United States.

Fill in the chart to rank the countries of Micronesia by population from largest to smallest. Then answer the questions at the bottom of this page.

Rank by Population	Country	Population
1		
2		
3		
4		
5		

1. The population of the largest country is about how much more than that of the smallest country? _____

2. Which two countries are the closest in population?

_____

Micronesia

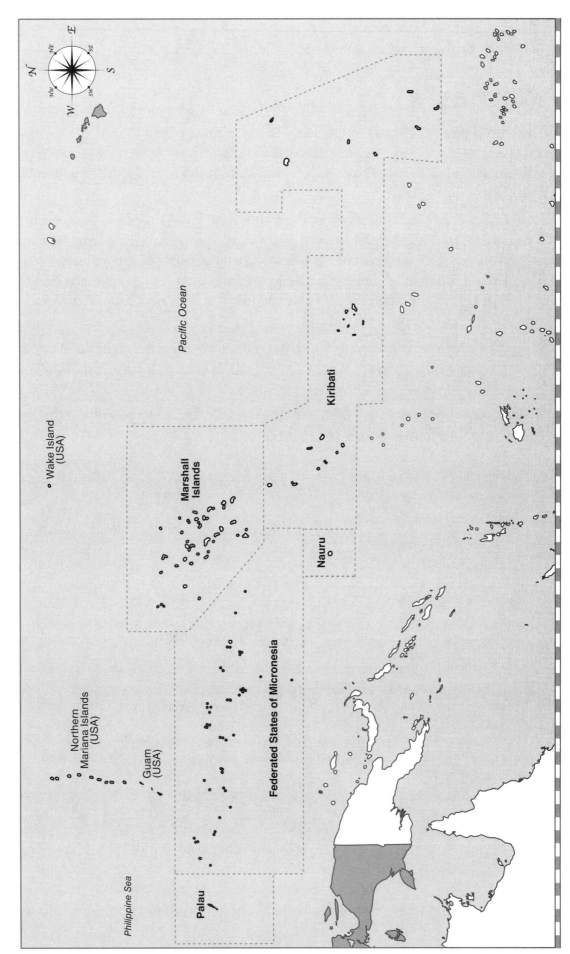

Wake Island
(USA)

Northern
Mariana Islands
(USA)

Guam
(USA)

Palau

Philippine Sea

Federated States of Micronesia

**Marshall
Islands**

Kiribati

Nauru

Pacific Ocean

Name _____

Polynesia

The word *Polynesia* means "many islands." The hundreds of islands of Polynesia are located mostly southeast of Melanesia and Micronesia. Polynesia stretches from tiny Midway Island in the northeast to New Zealand in the south, spanning about 5,000 miles (8,000 km).

New Zealand is by far the largest of the four countries of Polynesia in terms of landmass. It consists of two large islands: North Island and South Island. The much smaller country of Tonga is located northeast of New Zealand and consists of 170 small islands, only 36 of which are inhabited. Samoa is located north of Tonga. Samoa is made up of the two islands of Upolu and Savaii. Most of the population lives on Upolu. Northwest of Samoa are the nine tiny islands of Tuvalu.

Several territories are located in Polynesia, including French Polynesia, American Samoa, Cook Islands, Midway Island, Niue, Pitcairn Islands Group, Tokelau, and Wallis and Futuna.

A. Complete each sentence by unscrambling the word or words under the line. Use the information above to help you.

1. Upolu is an island in the country of _____.
   maosa

2. _____ is a dependent territory of New Zealand.
   leakuto

3. _____ is made up of 170 small islands.
   gotan

4. _____ is northwest of Samoa.
   lauvut

5. The largest country in Polynesia is _____.
   ewn nalzade

6. The word _____ means "many islands."
   sinopealy

7. Tonga is _____ of Samoa.
   hotus

8. _____ is located about 5,000 miles from New Zealand.
   wamidy snaldi

B. On the map on the other page, circle the countries in red and the territories in blue.

Polynesia

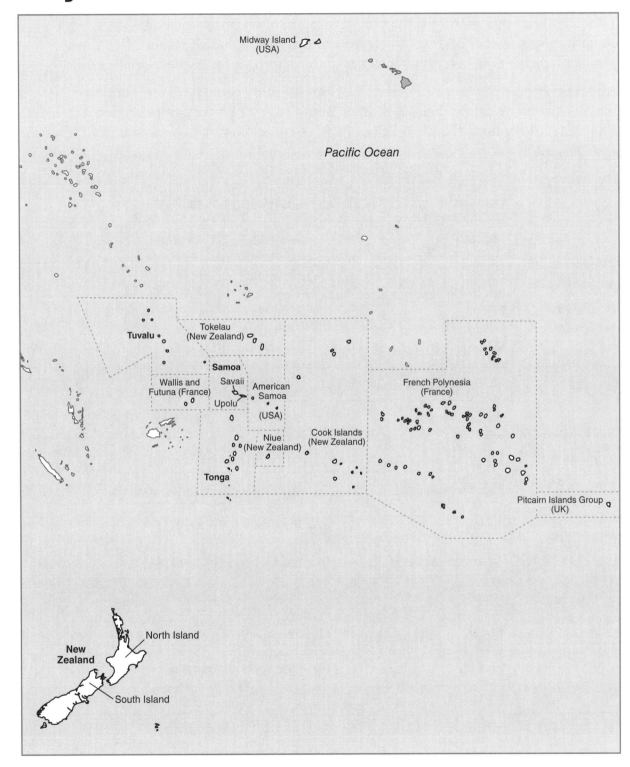

Midway Island
(USA)

Pacific Ocean

Tuvalu

Tokelau
(New Zealand)

Samoa

Wallis and
Futuna (France)

Savaii

Upolu

American
Samoa

(USA)

French Polynesia
(France)

Niue
(New Zealand)

Cook Islands
(New Zealand)

Tonga

Pitcairn Islands Group
(UK)

North Island

**New
Zealand**

South Island

Capital Cities of Australia and Oceania

The capital city of a country is the central location of its government. A capital city contains government buildings where leaders meet and laws are made. Often the president, prime minister, or other leader of the country lives in the capital city.

Almost every country has a capital city. In fact, the only country in the world that does not have a capital city is the tiny island nation of Nauru in Micronesia. The chart below shows the capital cities of all the other countries in Australia and Oceania.

Country	Region	Capital City
Australia	Australia	Canberra
Fiji	Melanesia	Suva
Kiribati	Micronesia	Tarawa
Marshall Islands	Micronesia	Majuro
Federated States of Micronesia	Micronesia	Palikir
New Zealand	Polynesia	Wellington
Palau	Micronesia	Melekeok
Papua New Guinea	Melanesia	Port Moresby
Samoa	Polynesia	Apia
Solomon Islands	Melanesia	Honiara
Tonga	Polynesia	Nukualofa
Tuvalu	Polynesia	Funafuti
Vanuatu	Melanesia	Port Vila

Capital Cities of Australia and Oceania

A. Use the chart on the other page to write the capital city of each of the 10 countries below.

Marshall
Islands: _____

Papua
New Guinea: _____

Australia: _____

Vanuatu: _____

Palau: _____

Samoa: _____

Kiribati: _____

New Zealand: _____

Fiji: _____

Tuvalu: _____

B. Find the 10 capital cities you wrote above in the word puzzle. Words may appear across, down, or diagonally.

```
P  O  R  T  M  O  R  E  S  B  Y  F  R
L  P  A  L  I  A  I  R  A  U  V  U  W
U  Y  E  X  B  T  D  A  B  C  V  N  E
C  M  Y  U  E  O  R  U  P  A  M  A  L
Y  P  S  L  E  H  C  A  R  N  I  F  L
M  E  L  E  K  E  O  K  S  B  O  U  I
S  C  N  P  L  A  M  N  C  E  T  T  N
N  U  K  U  A  L  P  F  A  R  W  I  G
M  A  J  U  R  O  V  I  D  R  S  A  T
E  D  T  A  R  A  W  A  A  A  P  O  O
Y  N  A  E  P  O  R  T  V  I  L  A  N
S  T  R  M  H  O  N  I  M  R  A  L  X
```

Name _____

Review

Use the words from the box to complete the crossword puzzle.

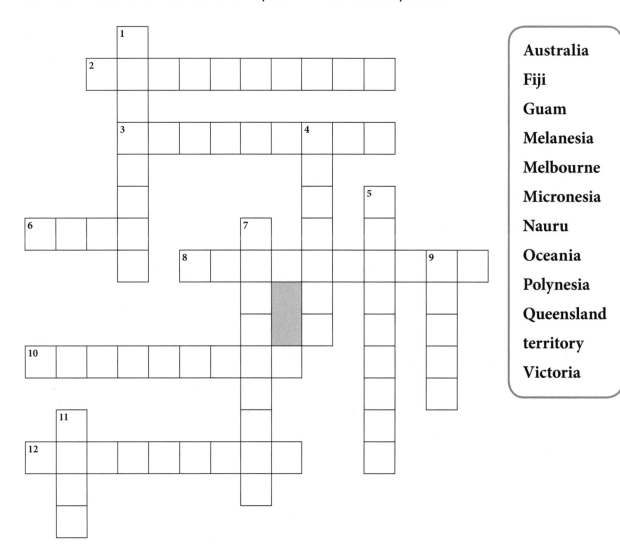

Australia

Fiji

Guam

Melanesia

Melbourne

Micronesia

Nauru

Oceania

Polynesia

Queensland

territory

Victoria

Across

2. a region made up of tiny islands

3. a place governed by another country

6. the fifth-largest country in Australia and Oceania

8. Brisbane is in this Australian state

10. the second-largest city in Australia

12. the only country that is also a continent

Down

1. one of the most populated states of Australia

4. an area made up of 30,000 islands

5. _____ means "many islands."

7. the region of Oceania that includes Papua New Guinea

9. the smallest country in Oceania

11. a territory of the United States

Physical Features of Australia and Oceania

In this section, students learn about the landforms and bodies of water of Australia and Oceania. Students discover that Australia is home to some of the most interesting landforms on Earth, including Uluru and the Great Barrier Reef. They learn about Australia's vast, hot deserts and Oceania's mountains and rainforests. Students also become familiar with the oceans, seas, and bays that surround Australia and Oceania.

Each skill in this section is based on the following National Geography Standards:

Essential Element 2: Places and Regions

Standard 4: The physical and human characteristics of places

Essential Element 3: Physical Systems

Standards 7 & 8: The physical processes that shape the patterns of Earth's surface, and the characteristics and spatial distribution of ecosystems on Earth's surface

CONTENTS

Overview

Because there are no other continents anywhere near it, Australia is the only continent that looks like a giant island. Its closest neighbors are New Zealand, Papua New Guinea, and the thousands of small islands that make up Oceania, which are all located in the Pacific Ocean.

Landforms

Australia is known for its vast, remote areas. Together these areas are called the Outback and they include several deserts, which cover about one-third of the continent. There are five major deserts in Australia: Great Sandy Desert, Great Victoria Desert, Gibson Desert, Simpson Desert, and Tanami Desert. In some desert areas, rows of long sand dunes stretch for up to 100 miles (161 km).

Not all of Australia is dry, however. Rainforests can also be found on the continent, and they are a common feature on many of the islands in Oceania. These islands include Fiji, New Zealand, and Papua New Guinea.

Perhaps the most unique landform of Australia and Oceania is the Great Barrier Reef. The Great Barrier Reef is a large system of coral that grows in the Coral Sea off the coast of Australia. Coral also helps to form some of the islands of Oceania, such as Kiribati and Tuvalu. Other islands in Oceania, such as New Zealand and Fiji, were formed by volcanoes.

There are very few mountain ranges on Australia. Australia's largest mountain range, the Great Dividing Range, contains the tallest mountain on the continent, Mount Kosciuszko. This mountain is 7,310 feet (2,228 m) high. But there are many taller mountains in Oceania. New Zealand's Southern Alps contain hundreds of high peaks. However, the tallest mountains are in Papua New Guinea. At 14,793 feet (4,509 m), Mount Wilhelm is the tallest mountain in the Australia/Oceania region.

Bodies of Water

Australia is bordered by the Indian and Pacific oceans, as well as by many seas. Several of these seas are joined together by *straits,* which are narrow channels of water that connect larger bodies of water. The Great Australian Bight, a large bay, defines the continent's southern coast.

Although there are no permanent natural lakes in the Australian Outback, there are many lake beds that fill with water after heavy rains. The largest of these lakes is Lake Eyre in South Australia. There are also many riverbeds in Australia that are dry for months of the year. The largest river in Australia that does flow year-round is the Murray River.

New Zealand and all of the other islands of Oceania are surrounded entirely by the Pacific Ocean. An interesting feature of New Zealand is its giant *fjords,* or narrow inlets of sea, that make deep cuts into the southwestern coast of the country's South Island.

Overview

Fill in the bubble to answer each question.

1. Which statement about Mount Wilhelm is true?

    Ⓐ Mount Wilhelm is located in the Great Dividing Range.

    Ⓑ Mount Wilhelm is the tallest mountain in Australia and Oceania.

    Ⓒ Mount Wilhelm is 7,310 feet tall.

    Ⓓ Mount Wilhelm is located in New Zealand.

2. Which of these is *not* a desert in Australia?

    Ⓐ Great Sandy Desert

    Ⓑ Simpson Desert

    Ⓒ Outback Desert

    Ⓓ Gibson Desert

3. Which of these islands were formed by a volcano?

    Ⓐ Tuvalu

    Ⓑ Fiji

    Ⓒ Kiribati

    Ⓓ Australia

4. Which two oceans border Australia?

    Ⓐ Atlantic and Pacific

    Ⓑ Pacific and Arctic

    Ⓒ Atlantic and Indian

    Ⓓ Indian and Pacific

5. Which statement about the lakes and rivers of Australia is true?

    Ⓐ All of the lakes and rivers are always dry.

    Ⓑ Most of the lakes and some of the rivers are dry for part of the year.

    Ⓒ Most of the rivers and some of the lakes are dry for part of the year.

    Ⓓ All of the lakes and rivers are permanent.

Landscape of Australia and Oceania

The landscape of Australia and the islands of Oceania range from hot deserts to lush rainforests to snowcapped mountains. Deserts cover one-third of Australia. In fact, it is the second-driest continent in the world behind Antarctica. Off the northeastern coast of Australia is the Great Barrier Reef, which is so big that it can be seen from outer space. The continent also contains rainforests and mountains that cover the eastern coast.

Besides having beautiful sandy beaches, the islands of Oceania also contain rainforests and mountains. Some of the tallest mountains in the region are on Papua New Guinea and New Zealand.

A. Use the information above and the map on the other page to answer the questions.

1. In which country are the Southern Alps located? _____

2. Which Australian desert is located farthest south? _____

3. What is the name of the major peak in Papua New Guinea? _____

4. Which landform is located in the sea off the northeastern coast of Australia? _____

5. What is the name of the major peak in Australia? _____

6. Which Australian desert is located farthest east? _____

7. On which island nation is Mt. Cook located? _____

B. Color the map on the other page according to the directions below.

1. Color the mountains brown.

2. Color the island of Tasmania green.

3. Circle the names of the deserts in yellow.

4. Circle the Great Barrier Reef in blue.

The 7 Continents: Australia and Oceania • EMC 3733 • © Evan-Moor Corp.

Landscape of Australia and Oceania

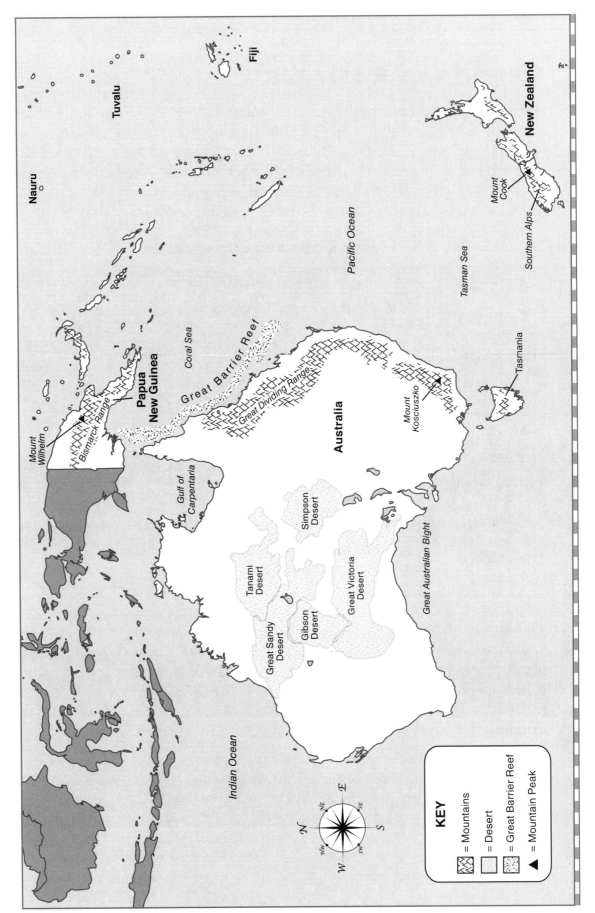

Fiji

Tuvalu

Nauru

New Zealand

Mount Cook

Southern Alps

Tasman Sea

Pacific Ocean

Papua New Guinea

Mount Wilhelm

Bismarck Range

Coral Sea

Great Barrier Reef

Great Dividing Range

Tasmania

Australia

Mount Kosciuszko

Gulf of Carpentaria

Simpson Desert

Tanami Desert

Great Sandy Desert

Gibson Desert

Great Victoria Desert

Great Australian Bight

Indian Ocean

KEY

= Mountains

= Desert

= Great Barrier Reef

▲ = Mountain Peak

N   NE   E   SE   S   SW   W   NW

Deserts of Australia

Australia contains vast areas of dry land where few people live. These areas are called the Outback. Some parts of the Outback have grasses, shrubs, and a few species of small trees, but much of the Outback is desert. In fact, a good portion of the land is covered in red sand dunes. In most areas there is not much rain, and what little rain does fall is often in the form of seasonal thunderstorms. In the summer, temperatures of over 100°F (38°C) are not uncommon. In some areas, temperatures can reach 120°F (49°C).

Five Major Deserts of Australia

Desert	Size	Interesting Facts
Gibson Desert	60,000 square miles (155,000 square km)	This desert consists mainly of gravel hills and dry grasses with areas of sandy dunes.
Great Sandy Desert	150,00 square miles (400,000 square km)	This desert is the second-largest desert in Australia. It contains rows of red sand dunes that are hundreds of miles long.
Great Victoria Desert	250,000 square miles (647,000 square km)	This desert is the largest desert in Australia. It is made up of small sand hills and areas of gravel. There are also salt lakes.
Simpson Desert	56,000 square miles (145,000 square km)	Located farthest east, this desert is dominated by large red sand dunes that can be up to 100 miles (161 km) long. It is home to the largest dune, nicknamed Big Red, which is over 130 feet (40 m) high.
Tanami Desert	71,000 square miles (184,000 square km)	Located in the Northern Territory, this desert is considered to be one of the most isolated places on Earth. It is made up mostly of sandy plains with low grasses and shrubs.

The deserts are home to many animals that have adapted to the harsh environment. Snakes thrive in the heat, as do lizards such as bearded dragons, geckos, and thorny devils. The bilby, a small marsupial, spends the hot daytime deep underground and comes out only during the cooler nights. Other small mammals, such as the hopping mouse, also burrow to keep cool. Birds such as parrots, owls, and hawks fly long distances to find water.

Unfortunately, many desert animals are endangered or have already gone extinct. This is due to competition with *nonnative* animals, or animals that people have brought to the Australian deserts. Cats, foxes, rabbits, and even camels now compete with native animals for food.

Deserts of Australia

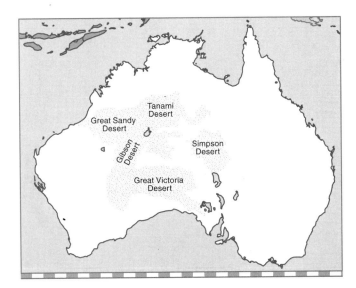

A. Use the map above and the information on the other page to answer the questions.

1. What are the areas of Australia where few people live sometimes called? _____

2. In which desert can you find salt lakes? _____

3. Which desert is the second-largest in Australia? _____

4. Which desert is 60,000 square miles in size? _____

5. Which desert contains a dune called Big Red? _____

6. Why do some animals burrow underground in the desert?

_____

B. Pretend you are going to visit a desert in the Outback. Name six things—landforms, plants, or animals—that you might see.

_____   _____

_____   _____

_____   _____

Uluru/Ayers Rock

Uluru, also called Ayers Rock, is a large rock formation located in the Tanami Desert in the Northern Territory of Australia. It rises 1,100 feet (335 m), only 150 feet (46 m) less than the Empire State Building. Uluru is over a mile and a half (2.4 km) long and a mile (1.6 km) wide. If you were to hike all the way around the rock, you would make a 6-mile (9-km) loop. Uluru is actually even bigger than it looks. Most of the formation is underground.

Uluru is made from sandstone that appears to change color throughout the day. It is especially beautiful at sunrise and sunset when it glows red. The base of the rock contains many shallow caves that have paintings and sculptures made by *Aboriginal* people, or people who are native to Australia. These caves, as well as the rock itself, are sacred to several Aboriginal tribes.

Uluru belongs to the Anungu, an Aboriginal tribe. The tribe has loaned the rock back to the Australian government to be part of the national park system. Even though the rock is located 280 miles (450 km) from Alice Springs, the nearest town, it is still a popular tourist destination. Up to half a million people visit Uluru each year. Because Uluru is a sacred place to the Anungu, they ask that tourists not climb it. However, the Australian government still allows people to climb the rock, and many do.

A. Would you like to visit Uluru? Why or why not?

_____

_____

_____

Uluru/Ayers Rock

B. Read each clue below and write the correct word or words on the numbered lines. Then use the numbers to crack the code!

1. Uluru is located in Australia's ____ Territory.

$\overline{24}$ $\overline{23}$ $\overline{20}$ $\overline{18}$ $\overline{4}$ $\overline{7}$ $\overline{20}$ $\overline{24}$

2. Uluru is sacred to some ____ tribes.

$\overline{11}$ $\overline{10}$ $\overline{23}$ $\overline{20}$ $\overline{3}$ $\overline{5}$ $\overline{3}$ $\overline{24}$ $\overline{11}$ $\overline{26}$

3. Uluru is made from ____.

$\overline{19}$ $\overline{11}$ $\overline{24}$ $\overline{8}$ $\overline{19}$ $\overline{18}$ $\overline{23}$ $\overline{24}$ $\overline{7}$

4. There are many shallow ____ in Uluru.

$\overline{9}$ $\overline{11}$ $\overline{16}$ $\overline{7}$ $\overline{19}$

5. The ____ tribe owns Uluru.

$\overline{11}$ $\overline{24}$ $\overline{17}$ $\overline{24}$ $\overline{5}$ $\overline{17}$

6. The closest town to Uluru is ____.

$\overline{11}$ $\overline{26}$ $\overline{3}$ $\overline{9}$ $\overline{7}$ $\quad$ $\overline{19}$ $\overline{22}$ $\overline{20}$ $\overline{3}$ $\overline{24}$ $\overline{5}$ $\overline{19}$

Crack the Code!

When it rains at Uluru, the rock can appear ____ in color.

$\overline{19}$ $\overline{3}$ $\overline{26}$ $\overline{16}$ $\overline{7}$ $\overline{20}$

The Great Barrier Reef

The Great Barrier Reef, which runs along the northeastern coast of Australia, is the largest coral reef system in the world. Coral reefs are made from tiny animals called *polyps* that have a hard outer skeleton. Over time, millions of polyps growing together can form a reef. The Great Barrier Reef is about 1,400 miles (2,300 km) long. In some places it is only about 10 miles (16 km) off the coast of Australia, while in others it is 100 miles (160 km) away.

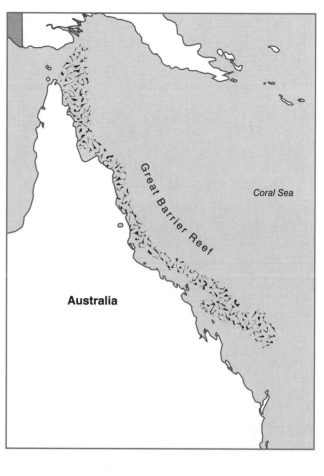

Great Barrier Reef

Coral Sea

Australia

Fast Facts About the Great Barrier Reef

- The Great Barrier Reef is made up of over 3,000 islets, or small islands, and reefs.

- Over 300 species of polyps make up the Great Barrier Reef.

- The Great Barrier Reef has been growing for millions of years.

- The Great Barrier Reef is home to many marine animals, including anemones, sponges, worms, lobsters, prawns, and crabs. They feast on red and green algae that cover much of the reef.

- Over 1,500 different kinds of fish live on the Great Barrier Reef. Most of these are small colorful fish. The largest fish on the reef is the whale shark, which can grow to be 39 feet (12 m) long.

- There are over 200 species of birds that live on the islets of the reef. They are attracted to the reef by the many fish and shellfish they can find and eat there.

- Six of the seven species of sea turtles in the world live on the Great Barrier Reef.

- One of the greatest natural threats to the reef is the crown-of-thorns starfish, a type of sea star, which eats the coral. The population of this sea star increased dramatically in the 1960s. Scientists think this is because people began collecting the beautiful shell of a giant sea snail called the Pacific triton, the biggest predator of the crown-of-thorns starfish.

The Great Barrier Reef

A. Complete each sentence by unscrambling the word or words under the line. Use the information on the other page to help you.

1. Six species of _____ live on the Great Barrier Reef.
   esa letturs

2. The Great Barrier Reef is about 2,300 _____ long.
   skimetorel

3. The Great Barrier Reef is located off the _____ coast
   of Australia.
   renshenaortt

4. Red and green _____ provide food for fish on the reef.
   galea

5. The _____ is the largest fish that lives on the reef.
   lehaw rahks

6. More than 200 species of _____ live along the reef.
   drisb

7. The _____ is collected for its shell.
   cafpici nirtot

8. A coral reef is made from the skeletons of coral _____.
   sloppy

9. The Great Barrier Reef has been growing for _____ of years.
   limilosn

10. The reef is home to marine animals such as _____.
    samenone

B. Why do you think there are so many animals that live on the Great Barrier Reef?

_____

_____

_____

Islands of Oceania

Coral reefs not only make up the Great Barrier Reef, but they also help form many of the islands in Oceania. Those islands not formed by coral reefs were created by underwater volcanic eruptions.

Coral Reef Islands

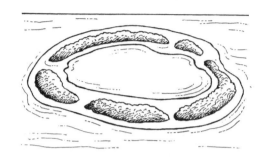

Some islands in Oceania were formed from coral reefs made of the skeletons of millions of tiny sea creatures. Coral reefs become islands when the sea level drops below the reef, or the land beneath the reef rises. Over time, dust and sand collect on top of the reef, forming the land of the island. Coral islands are usually just a few feet above sea level, which is why they are sometimes called "low islands." Coral islands in Oceania include Kiribati, Tuvalu, French Polynesia, and Nauru.

One type of coral island formation is called an *atoll*. When a volcanic island sinks to the ocean floor, the coral reef surrounding the island will grow upward, forming a ring of small islands, or *islets,* around a shallow body of water called a *lagoon.* The largest atoll in the world is Kwajalein, located in the Marshall Islands. It contains 90 islets around a 839 square mile (2,173 square km) lagoon.

Volcanic Islands

Many of the islands of Oceania are volcanic islands. Volcanic islands form from volcanoes that erupt under the water. The volcano spews lava, which is deposited on the ocean floor and cools. Over time, the volcanic eruptions build up layers of lava until it breaks through the surface of the water. The cooled lava then becomes an island. Volcanic islands are sometimes called "high islands" because they can rise high above the ocean's surface.

Some of the islands in Oceania that were formed by volcanoes include New Zealand, Fiji, Vanuatu, Samoa, and the Solomon Islands. Many of these islands still contain active volcanoes. Volcanoes that have erupted recently include Ulawun in Papua New Guinea, Gaua in Vanuatu, and Tinakula in the Solomon Islands.

Islands of Oceania

Circle the correct word or words to complete each sentence. Use information on the other page to help you.

1. Fiji is made up of ____ islands.

   coral   **volcanic**   **atoll**

2. Islands that were formed by volcanoes are sometimes called ____ islands.

   low   **medium**   **high**

3. A small island is called a(n) ____.

   atoll   **islet**   **lagoon**

4. Underwater volcanoes deposit ____ on the ocean floor.

   lava   **coral**   **ash**

5. ____ is a volcanic island.

   Kwajalein   **Nauru**   **Vanuatu**

6. ____ is a coral island.

   Tuvalu   **Samoa**   **Fiji**

7. Kwajalein in the Marshall Islands is the world's largest ____.

   volcano   **atoll**   **island**

8. ____ is an active volcano in the Solomon Islands.

   Ulawun   **Gaua**   **Tinakula**

9. Volcanic islands are formed by ____.

   underwater eruptions   **sinking volcanoes**   **skeletons of sea creatures**

Mountains

While not the tallest in the world, the mountains in Australia and Oceania are still majestic landforms. There are three major mountain systems in Australia and Oceania.

Bismarck Range

The Bismarck Range, located in Papua New Guinea, is home to the tallest mountain in the Australia/Oceania region—Mount Wilhelm. Mount Wilhelm is 14,793 feet (4,509 m) high. Many other tall mountains are also located in the Bismarck Range, which stretches for 280 miles (450 km). The tops of the tallest mountains are usually blanketed in snow, while the lower slopes are covered in dense rainforest.

The Southern Alps

The dramatic slopes of the Southern Alps are located on the South Island of New Zealand. They stretch 360 miles (579 km) down the entire length of the island. The Southern Alps have hundreds of mountains over 7,000 feet (2,134 m) tall and 16 mountains that are over 10,000 feet (3,048 m) tall. The tallest mountain in the Southern Alps is Mount Cook, also called Aoraki, at 12,316 feet (3,754 m). Mount Cook, like the other tall mountains in the Southern Alps, is covered with cold, icy glaciers. There are at least 3,000 glaciers in the Southern Alps.

The Great Dividing Range

Although Australia is a mostly flat country, it has one system of mountains that spans the eastern edge of the continent. This system is called the Great Dividing Range and is actually made up of several mountain ranges. It stretches 2,300 miles (3,700 km) through the states of Queensland, New South Wales, and Victoria. Although long, the Great Dividing Range is not high. Most of the range is made up of plateaus and low mountains. Few are taller than 3,000 feet (900 m). The tallest mountain in the Great Dividing Range is Mount Kosciuszko, which is 7,310 feet (2,228 m) high.

A. Fill in the chart for each mountain. Use the information above to help you.

Mountain	Height in Feet	Mountain Range	Country
Mt. Cook			
Mt. Kosciuszko			
Mt. Wilhelm			

Mountains

B. Label the three mountain ranges on the map. Use the information on the other page to help you.

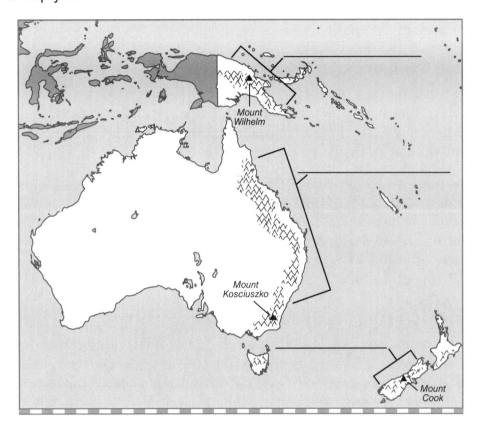

C. Write the letter of the clue that describes each number. Use the information on the other page to help you.

_____ 1. 360 miles   a. the length of the Bismarck Mountain Range

_____ 2. 14,793 feet   b. the minimum number of glaciers in the Southern Alps

_____ 3. 7,310 feet   c. the height of Mount Kosciuszko

_____ 4. 12,316 feet   d. the number of mountains over 10,000 feet in the Southern Alps

_____ 5. 280 miles

_____ 6. 16   e. the length of the Southern Alps

_____ 7. 3,000   f. the maximum height of most mountains in Australia

_____ 8. 3,000 feet   g. the height of the tallest mountain in Oceania

    h. the height of Mount Cook

Rainforests

The many rainforests of Australia and Oceania are home to thousands of different plant and animal species. The largest rainforests are in Papua New Guinea and New Zealand, but there are also rainforests in Australia, the Solomon Islands, Fiji, and many of the other small islands of Oceania.

Tropical and Temperate Rainforests

There are two different kinds of rainforests. *Tropical rainforests* are what most people think of when they hear the word *rainforest*. Tropical rainforests are found near the equator where it is always hot. A tropical rainforest contains thousands of different kinds of plants and animals.

Temperate rainforests are located farther from the equator where the temperature is cooler. Unlike tropical rainforests, which can be found inland, temperate rainforests are found only in coastal areas. Although there are not as many different kinds of plants and animals in a temperate rainforest as there are in a tropical one, there is still a great deal of life. The frequent rainfall creates a lush green environment where plants and animals thrive.

Tropical Rainforest in Papua New Guinea

Over 100,000 square miles (258,000 square km) of tropical rainforest can be found in Papua New Guinea. The forest contains over 20,000 different kinds of plants, including about 1,500 species of trees. These plants make ideal habitats for the more than 284 different types of mammals and the 750 species of birds that live there. Many of these animals cannot be found anywhere else in the world.

The rainforest of Papua New Guinea is home to the Queen Alexandra's Birdwing butterfly, which has a wingspan of up to 1 foot (30 cm), making it the world's largest butterfly. Another unique animal of this rainforest is the buff-faced pygmy parrot, the world's smallest parrot, which is only about the size of an adult human's thumb.

Temperate Rainforests in New Zealand

The South Island of New Zealand has about 25,000 square miles (65,000 square km) of temperate rainforests along the west coast of South Island, as well as on North Island. These forests contain over 700 different kinds of plants. There are many species of insects as well as many different kinds of birds. However, there are few other types of animals. There are no snakes and only a few species of reptiles, including a lizard-like reptile called a tuatara, which is found only in New Zealand. There are four species of frogs and two species of bats. Other than bats, there are no other native mammals in the rainforests of New Zealand.

Name _____

Rainforests

A. Read each statement. Circle **yes** if it is true or **no** if it is false. Use the information on the other page to help you.

1. Over 750 species of birds live in the rainforests of Papua New Guinea.   **Yes   No**

2. Temperate rainforests are located near the equator.   **Yes   No**

3. A tuatara is a type of large spider found in New Zealand.   **Yes   No**

4. There are no mammals native to New Zealand's rainforests.   **Yes   No**

5. There are rainforests on Fiji and the Solomon Islands.   **Yes   No**

6. There are only four species of frogs in New Zealand's rainforests.   **Yes   No**

7. The Queen Alexandra's Birdwing butterfly is the world's smallest butterfly.   **Yes   No**

8. Temperate rainforests receive very little rainfall.   **Yes   No**

9. The rainforest in Papua New Guinea contains more than 20,000 species of plants.   **Yes   No**

10. There are three species of snakes in New Zealand's rainforests.   **Yes   No**

B. List three ways that a temperate rainforest is different from a tropical rainforest.

1. _____

_____

2. _____

_____

3. _____

_____

Bodies of Water

Every country in Australia and Oceania, with the exception of Papua New Guinea, is completely surrounded by water. Australia is bordered to the south and west by the Indian Ocean and to the east by the Pacifc Ocean. The Timor Sea is northwest of Australia and the Arafura Sea borders the continent to the north. The Coral Sea is to the northeast of Australia. The Tasman Sea is located between Australia and New Zealand.

Other large bodies of water include the Great Australian Bight, which is a large bay that takes up most of the southern coast of Australia, and the Gulf of Carpentaria, which is on the north side of the continent. There are also several straits, which are narrow channels of water that join two larger bodies of water. The Torres Strait runs between the Arafura Sea and the Coral Sea. The Bass Strait is located between the Australian mainland and the island of Tasmania. And the Cook Strait divides the two islands of New Zealand.

A. Label the bodies of water on the map on the other page. Use the information above and the word box on the other page to help you.

B. Circle the correct answer for each clue. Use the information above and the map on the other page to help you.

1. the ocean west of Australia	**Pacific**	**Indian**
2. a country that is not completely surrounded by water	**New Zealand**	**Papua New Guinea**
3. a sea located southeast of Australia	**Tasman**	**Timor**
4. a sea located southwest of Papua New Guinea	**Coral**	**Arafura**
5. the strait that divides the islands of New Zealand	**Cook**	**Bass**
6. the strait that joins the Arafura and Coral seas	**Bass**	**Torres**
7. a large bay off Australia's southern coast	**Gulf of Carpentaria**	**Great Australian Bight**

C. What is a strait?

_____

_____

Bodies of Water

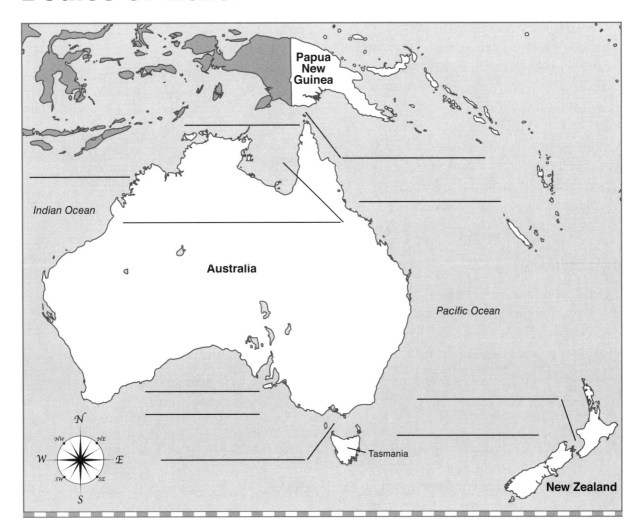

© Evan-Moor Corp. • EMC 3733 • The 7 Continents: Australia and Oceania

Seas	Bays and Gulfs	Straits
Arafura Sea	**Great Australian Bight**	**Bass Strait**
Coral Sea	**Gulf of Carpentaria**	**Cook Strait**
Tasman Sea		**Torres Strait**
Timor Sea		

Fjords of New Zealand

On the southwestern coast of New Zealand's South Island there is a beautiful region called Fjordland. This area is home to 14 *fjords*. A fjord is a long and narrow inlet of sea that cuts into the land. The fjords in New Zealand were formed around 20,000 years ago during the Ice Age. As glaciers flowed toward the sea, they cut narrow, U-shaped valleys into the land. When the Ice Age was over, these valleys filled with melted ice and seawater to create the fjords.

Fjords, unlike other kinds of inlets, are shallower near the entrance to the sea than they are farther inland. This is because the glaciers pushed debris toward the sea as they flowed away from the land. The fjords in New Zealand are about 330 feet (100 m) deep at their entrances and often over 1,300 feet (396 m) deep inland.

Although New Zealand's inlets are fjords, most of them have been named as *sounds*. A sound is another name for a body of water that reaches into the land.

A. Use the information above and the map on the other page to answer the questions.

1. Which fjord is farthest north in New Zealand?   _____

2. When were the fjords of New Zealand formed?   _____

3. What is a fjord?

   _____

4. How are fjords different from other kinds of inlets?

   _____

B. Write a caption for the map on the other page using at least two facts about fjords.

Name _____

Fjords of New Zealand

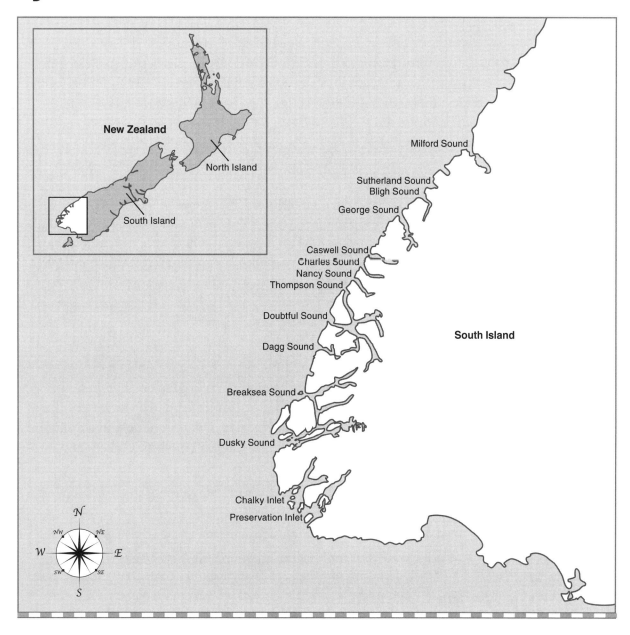

_____

_____

Lakes of Australia

Australia has a very dry climate. Much of the continent receives very little rainfall. Because of this, Australia does not have any large lakes that are filled with water year-round, except for those that were created artificially. Most natural lakes in Australia are dry for months or even years at a time. Since the dry lake beds are often made from salt, saltwater lakes are created when they fill after a heavy rain. The largest salt lakes in Australia include Lake Disappointment, Lake Eyre, Lake Frome, Lake Gairdner, Lake Mackay, and Lake Torrens.

The Largest Saltwater Lake

At 3,700 square miles (9,300 square km), Lake Eyre is the largest lake in Australia. It is also the lowest point on the continent at 50 feet (15 m) below sea level. Since Lake Eyre is located in one of the driest areas of the country, the lake fills only a few times each century. The last time the lake was completely full was in 1984. When the lake fills, it takes two years for it to dry up again. However, Lake Eyre does fill up partially much more often.

Freshwater Lakes

There are a few freshwater lakes in Australia. One type of freshwater lake is a glacial lake. A glacial lake is one that forms from the melted ice of a glacier. Blue Lake in the southeastern part of Australia is a glacial lake. Another type of freshwater lake in Australia is a crater lake. A crater lake forms when rainwater collects in a volcanic crater. Lake Barrine is a crater lake that is located in the far north of Queensland.

A. Read each statement. Circle **yes** if it is true or **no** if it is false. Use the information above to help you.

1. Large lakes in Australia are filled with water all year long.   **Yes**   **No**

2. Lake Eyre is the largest lake in Australia.   **Yes**   **No**

3. Lake Eyre fills with water only a few times every century.   **Yes**   **No**

4. The last time Lake Eyre was completely full was in 1994.   **Yes**   **No**

5. Crater lakes are saltwater lakes.   **Yes**   **No**

6. Glacial lakes form from melted ice.   **Yes**   **No**

Lakes of Australia

B. Use the map to find eight lakes of Australia. Then write the names of the lakes on the chart in alphabetical order.

Lake

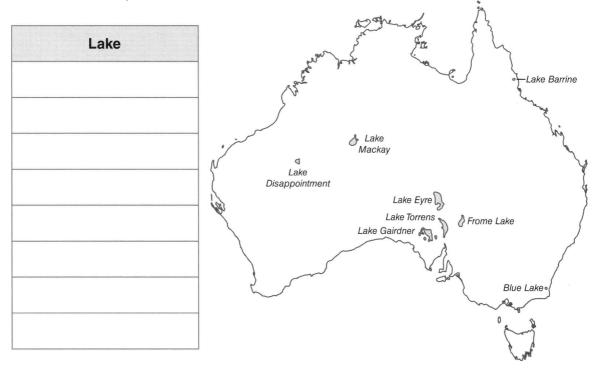

Lake Barrine

Lake Mackay

Lake Disappointment

Lake Eyre

Lake Torrens

Frome Lake

Lake Gairdner

Blue Lake

C. Find the names of the eight lakes from above in the word puzzle. Words may appear across, down, or diagonally.

```
T  H  S  Y  F  H  O  P  E  M  A  K  R  E  W
O  L  E  B  B  R  C  Y  M  E  X  L  E  U  L
D  I  S  A  P  P  O  I  N  T  M  E  N  T  E
A  W  H  R  D  O  G  M  A  L  A  O  G  A  H
V  E  T  R  A  E  Q  U  E  O  C  Y  A  R  C
I  O  K  I  I  H  W  O  L  A  K  D  I  E  A
D  A  R  N  B  O  T  U  C  E  A  I  R  L  R
L  I  F  E  A  L  I  K  N  O  Y  V  D  E  W
E  H  R  E  T  O  R  R  E  N  S  O  N  K  N
D  Y  A  D  A  Y  T  O  S  B  L  U  E  O  T
E  I  M  B  T  Y  C  U  L  H  Y  S  R  F  E
```

Rivers of Australia

Rivers are an important resource in Australia. They provide drinking water for people and animals as well as irrigation water for crops. Many of Australia's rivers are dry for part of the year. These rivers fill only during the rainy season, which is generally from December through March. Many of the rivers are dammed to create lakes called *reservoirs* that store water for the dry season.

The largest year-round river is the Murray River in southeastern Australia. The Murray River is 1,476 miles (2,375 km) long. It begins in the Snowy Mountains of New South Wales and winds its way west to end near the city of Adelaide. The Murray River has several *tributaries,* or smaller rivers, including the Darling and the Murrumbidgee rivers.

Longest Rivers in Australia

River	Length in Miles	Length in Kilometers
Cooper Creek	692	1,113
Darling River	915	1,472
Diamantina River	585	941
Flinders River	624	1,004
Lachlan River	832	1,339
Murray River	1,476	2,375
Murrumbidgee River	923	1,485

A. Use the information in the chart above to put the seven longest rivers of Australia in order from longest to shortest.

Rank in Length	River
1	
2	
3	
4	
5	
6	
7	

Rivers of Australia

B. Use the information on the other page to write a caption for the map.

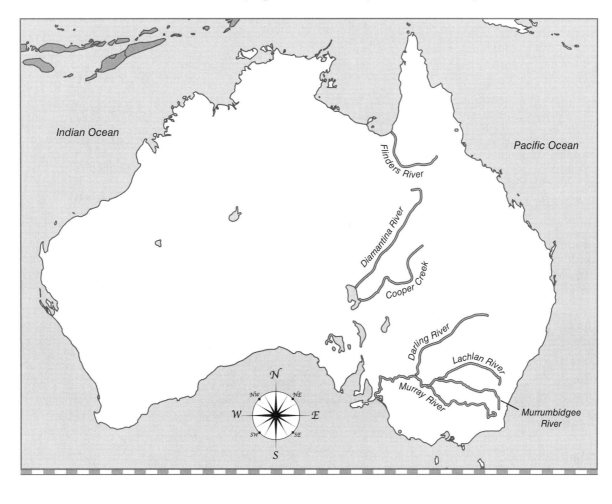

Indian Ocean

Pacific Ocean

Flinders River

Diamantina River

Cooper Creek

Darling River

Lachlan River

Murray River

Murrumbidgee River

N

NW   NE

W   E

SW   SE

S

_____

_____

_____

Review

Use words from the box to complete the crossword puzzle.

fjords
Murray
Outback
sandstone
starfish
Tasman
temperate
Wilhelm

Across

1. The _____ is another name for the huge, remote areas of Australia.

4. Mount _____ is the tallest mountain in Australia and Oceania.

6. Uluru is made from _____ rock.

7. The _____ of New Zealand were formed by glaciers.

Down

2. The _____ Sea is located between Australia and New Zealand.

3. _____ rainforests are located near the coast of New Zealand.

5. The _____ River is the longest permanent river in Australia.

6. The crown-of-thorns _____ is a threat to the Great Barrier Reef.

Valuable Resources of Australia and Oceania

In this section, students learn about the various natural resources of Australia and Oceania. They discover that mining is an important industry in Australia and Papua New Guinea. Students also learn about important regional crops and livestock and are introduced to some of the challenges of managing a large tourism industry. In addition, students learn about the interesting animals of Australia and Oceania.

Each skill in this section is based on the following National Geography Standards:

Essential Element 3: Physical Systems

Standard 8: The characteristics and spatial distribution of ecosystems on Earth's surface

Essential Element 5: Environment and Society

Standard 14: How human actions modify the physical environment

Standard 16: The changes that occur in the meaning, use, distribution, and importance of resources

CONTENTS

Overview

Natural resources are the minerals, plants, animals, and other elements that humans use from their environment. Australia and Oceania are rich in many kinds of natural resources, especially metal and mineral deposits. Large numbers of sheep and cattle are raised in Australia and New Zealand. Fishing and tourism are important industries in Oceania. And the Australia/Oceania region is home to many animals that are unique to the continent and its surrounding islands.

Energy

Australia has huge reserves of coal. Over three-fourths of Australia's electricity comes from coal. In New Zealand, where there are many rivers, most of the electricity comes from *hydropower*. Hydropower is generated from the force of flowing water.

Farming

Grapes are an important crop in Australia. The country has a thriving wine industry, and vineyards can be found in every state. Wheat, cotton, and sugarcane are also important crops for Australia, but these crops can be grown only in the east where there is enough water. Small farms on the islands of Oceania grow fruit, coconuts, sugar, and other small crops, too.

Livestock are another significant part of the region's economy. Huge cattle and sheep ranches called *stations* can be found in both Australia and New Zealand.

Fishing

Many people in Oceania make their living by fishing. Fish are caught to sell at the local markets and to export to other countries. Foreign fishing boats must pay large fees to fish in Oceania's waters. Many different types of fish are caught in Oceania, including several kinds of tuna.

Tourism

The tourism industry is essential to many of the small islands in Oceania. People come to these islands to enjoy the beautiful beaches, see the rainforests, and learn about the people who live there. *Ecotourism,* which is a form of tourism that emphasizes protection of the environment, is growing in Oceania.

Wildlife

Australia is known for its large populations of *marsupials*. These animals, which include kangaroos, wallabies, koalas, and Tasmanian devils, all carry their young in a pouch. New Zealand, however, is known for having no native mammals other than bats. But it does have many birds, including the small, flightless kiwi, which is the national bird of New Zealand.

Overview

Fill in the bubble to answer each question or complete each sentence.

1. By what means is most of the electricity in New Zealand produced?

   Ⓐ coal

   Ⓑ wind

   Ⓒ water

   Ⓓ oil

2. What are two important crops in Australia?

   Ⓐ sugarcane and coconuts

   Ⓑ wheat and coconuts

   Ⓒ kiwi and sugarcane

   Ⓓ wheat and cotton

3. Large sheep and cattle ranches in Australia and New Zealand are called _____.

   Ⓐ stations

   Ⓑ ports

   Ⓒ vineyards

   Ⓓ eco farms

4. Fishing boats from other parts of the world _____.

   Ⓐ must give half their catch to the countries in Oceania

   Ⓑ must pay large fees to fish in Oceania's waters

   Ⓒ are not allowed to fish in Oceania

   Ⓓ do not catch tuna

5. Which of these animals is *not* a marsupial?

   Ⓐ kiwi

   Ⓑ Tasmanian devil

   Ⓒ koala

   Ⓓ wallaby

Coal in Australia

Australia is rich in coal, which is a kind of *fossil fuel* that is formed from decaying plant matter. Fossil fuels take millions of years to form, so they are a limited resource on Earth.

There are coal deposits in every state of the country. However, New South Wales and Queensland are by far the largest producers of coal. Depending on where the coal is found, it is mined in one of two ways. Coal that is deep underground must be mined through tunnels that are dug to reach the coal. Machines do most of the digging and loading. Coal that is close to the surface of the ground, however, is mined by using explosives and giant earth-moving machines to remove the soil covering the deposit. Then the exposed coal is loaded into large trucks. This kind of mining is called *open cut,* or *strip mining.*

Australia exports a great deal of coal to other countries. In fact, Australia is the world's largest exporter of coal. The continent is also dependent on coal for almost all of its electricity. Over 78% of the electricity that Australia uses comes from burning coal. Unfortunately, burning coal causes pollution, which contributes to global warming. Also, strip mining can do a lot of damage to the land and create erosion problems.

Australia's Coal Deposits

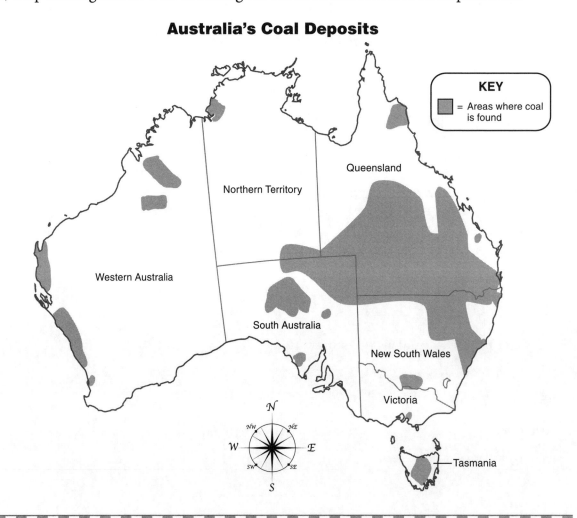

KEY

■ = Areas where coal is found

Queensland

Northern Territory

Western Australia

South Australia

New South Wales

Victoria

Tasmania

Coal in Australia

A. Read each statement. Circle **yes** if it is true or **no** if it is false. Use the information and map on the other page to help you.

1. There are coal deposits in every state of Australia.   Yes   No

2. Australia exports more coal than any other country.   Yes   No

3. Most of Australia's coal deposits are in the west.   Yes   No

4. Explosives are never used to mine coal in Australia.   Yes   No

5. Coal is a limited resource.   Yes   No

6. Burning coal does not cause pollution.   Yes   No

7. Coal is located in the southwest corner of the Northern Territory.   Yes   No

8. Over 87% of Australia's electricity comes from coal.   Yes   No

9. The state with the most coal is Queensland.   Yes   No

10. Coal is always found close to the surface.   Yes   No

B. Answer the questions. Use the information and map on the other page to help you.

1. Which state has the least amount of coal?   _____

2. Why are fossil fuels a limited resource?

   _____

3. What are two problems associated with depending on coal for electricity?

   _____

   _____

Hydroelectricity in New Zealand

With its many rivers, New Zealand is an ideal place for using water to generate electricity. This type of electricity is called hydropower, or hydroelectricity. Hydropower uses the force of falling water to spin machines called *turbines*. The motion of the spinning turbines then generates electricity. Today, hydropower supplies about 55% of New Zealand's electricity.

The first step in generating hydroelectricity from a river is to build a dam. The dam creates a lake called a *reservoir*, where the water is stored until it is needed. A single river can have several dams built along its course.

The Manapouri Hydropower Station

The Manapouri Hydropower Station is the largest hydropower plant in New Zealand. Rather than using river water that is stored behind a dam, the Manapouri plant uses water from Lake Manapouri, the second-deepest lake in New Zealand.

The power plant was built under a mountain. Workers dug through solid rock to build the *hall,* an area where the turbines are housed. Water enters the power plant through grates at the lake level. The water then drops down through large pipes called *penstocks* to the hall where its power spins the turbines. After the water is used to spin the turbines, it is carried to the sea through two long tunnels.

New Zealand

North Island

South Island

Manapouri Hydropower Station

A. Fill in the blanks to complete the paragraph. Use the information above to help you.

New Zealand's largest hydropower plant uses water from Lake

_____. The power station is unusual because it is built

under a _____. Workers had to dig through solid rock to

carve out an area for the _____, where the turbines are

located. Water reaches the turbines from the lake above through large pipes

called _____. Water is then carried away from the plant

through two tunnels that run to the _____.

Hydroelectricity in New Zealand

B. Read each clue below and write the correct word on the numbered lines. Then use the numbers to crack the code!

1. Hydropower uses the force of flowing water to spin ____.

$\overline{\hphantom{x}}$ $\overline{\hphantom{x}}$ $\overline{\hphantom{x}}$ $\overline{\hphantom{x}}$ $\overline{\hphantom{x}}$ $\overline{\hphantom{x}}$ $\overline{\hphantom{x}}$ $\overline{\hphantom{x}}$
11 12 9 19 26 5 22 10

2. Hydropower supplies about 55% of New Zealand's ____.

$\overline{\hphantom{x}}$ $\overline{\hphantom{x}}$ $\overline{\hphantom{x}}$ $\overline{\hphantom{x}}$ $\overline{\hphantom{x}}$ $\overline{\hphantom{x}}$ $\overline{\hphantom{x}}$ $\overline{\hphantom{x}}$ $\overline{\hphantom{x}}$ $\overline{\hphantom{x}}$ $\overline{\hphantom{x}}$
22 3 22 20 11 9 26 20 26 11 16

3. In most cases, the water for a hydropower plant comes from a ____.

$\overline{\hphantom{x}}$ $\overline{\hphantom{x}}$ $\overline{\hphantom{x}}$ $\overline{\hphantom{x}}$ $\overline{\hphantom{x}}$
9 26 13 22 9

4. When a river is dammed to make hydropower, it creates a lake called a ____.

$\overline{\hphantom{x}}$ $\overline{\hphantom{x}}$ $\overline{\hphantom{x}}$ $\overline{\hphantom{x}}$ $\overline{\hphantom{x}}$ $\overline{\hphantom{x}}$ $\overline{\hphantom{x}}$ $\overline{\hphantom{x}}$ $\overline{\hphantom{x}}$
9 22 10 22 9 13 6 26 9

5. The ____ Hydropower Station is the largest hydropower plant in New Zealand.

$\overline{\hphantom{x}}$ $\overline{\hphantom{x}}$ $\overline{\hphantom{x}}$ $\overline{\hphantom{x}}$ $\overline{\hphantom{x}}$ $\overline{\hphantom{x}}$ $\overline{\hphantom{x}}$ $\overline{\hphantom{x}}$ $\overline{\hphantom{x}}$
4 18 5 18 7 6 12 9 26

6. Water enters the power plant through ____.

$\overline{\hphantom{x}}$ $\overline{\hphantom{x}}$ $\overline{\hphantom{x}}$ $\overline{\hphantom{x}}$ $\overline{\hphantom{x}}$ $\overline{\hphantom{x}}$
2 9 18 11 22 10

Crack the Code!

The Manapouri turbines spin at a rate of 250 ____ per minute.

$\overline{\hphantom{x}}$ $\overline{\hphantom{x}}$ $\overline{\hphantom{x}}$ $\overline{\hphantom{x}}$ $\overline{\hphantom{x}}$ $\overline{\hphantom{x}}$ $\overline{\hphantom{x}}$ $\overline{\hphantom{x}}$ $\overline{\hphantom{x}}$ $\overline{\hphantom{x}}$ $\overline{\hphantom{x}}$
9 22 13 6 3 12 11 26 6 5 10

Mining Minerals

In addition to coal, Australia has a large number of metal and other mineral deposits. Unfortunately, most of these are located in the desert, far away from cities. This makes it very expensive to build and operate the mines. However, it is worth the cost. Australia makes a lot of money exporting gold, iron, opals, and many other minerals to other countries. In fact, about one-third of Australia's export dollars are from the mining industry.

Papua New Guinea also exports gold and copper. About 75% of the country's export dollars come from mining.

Minerals Mined in Australia and Oceania

Mineral	Where Mined	Fast Facts
bauxite	Australia, New Zealand	• used to make aluminum • found in cement, cosmetics, soda cans, and house siding • Australia produces more bauxite than any other country.
copper	Australia, Papua New Guinea	• used to make cookware, coins, electrical wires, and bronze
gold	Australia, New Zealand, Papua New Guinea, Fiji, Solomon Islands	• used in medical equipment, electronics, jewelry, artwork, and coins • Australia is one of the world's largest suppliers. • Papua New Guinea has one of the world's largest gold deposits.
iron	Australia	• used to make steel for construction of buildings, bridges, cars, and ships • used in appliances, tools, knives, and nails • Australia is one of the world's leading suppliers.
nickel	Australia, Solomon Islands	• used for making stainless steel because it does not rust • stainless steel used in cookware, appliances, tableware, and jewelry
opal	Australia	• The opal is the national gemstone of Australia. • Australia supplies 90% of the world's opals.
uranium	Australia	• a radioactive substance used to generate electricity and to make nuclear weapons • Australia has the world's largest reserves and is the third-largest producer.
zinc	Australia	• used in cars, toys, pipes, roofing, and batteries • often found near lead and silver deposits

Mining Minerals

A. Next to each mineral, write the letter of the clue that describes it. Use the information on the other page to help you.

_____ 1. bauxite

_____ 2. copper

_____ 3. zinc

_____ 4. opal

_____ 5. iron

_____ 6. nickel

_____ 7. gold

_____ 8. uranium

a. used mostly to make steel for construction

b. used for generating electricity

c. used to make electrical wires

d. mined in Australia, Papua New Guinea, New Zealand, Fiji, and the Solomon Islands

e. often found with lead and silver

f. used to make aluminum

g. Australia's national gem

h. mined only in Australia and the Solomon Islands

B. Find and circle each of the eight minerals listed above in the word puzzle below. Then find the names of three countries mentioned in the chart on the other page and circle them in red. Words may appear across, down, or diagonally.

```
W  E  F  I  J  I  N  G  R  P  L  R  I  W
A  L  N  Y  T  O  I  G  A  O  S  A  U  D
N  A  G  O  L  D  C  O  C  L  T  D  R  N
E  T  N  P  A  T  K  R  H  C  L  R  A  A
W  E  O  A  M  D  E  L  N  E  T  S  N  X
Z  M  V  L  E  A  L  O  L  R  C  M  I  S
E  C  H  Z  E  V  R  O  R  N  A  E  U  N
A  R  O  I  J  I  F  E  I  D  N  O  M  P
L  F  L  P  E  D  P  Z  A  M  I  A  C  E
A  L  U  C  P  M  I  K  E  W  L  A  U  U
N  Y  C  U  L  E  B  A  U  X  I  T  E  Q
D  O  A  U  S  T  R  A  L  I  A  P  E  D
```

Agriculture in Australia

Because much of Australia is covered by desert, most of the land is not good for growing crops. And the land that could be used for farming is instead used for raising livestock. Only about 10% of Australia's land, in fact, is farmed. Even with this limited amount of cropland, Australia grows enough food to feed its population and still has enough left over to export it to other countries.

Farms in Australia are very large, and machines are used to do most of the work. Major crops include wheat, sugarcane, and cotton. Recently, vineyards that produce grapes for making wine have also become important to Australia's economy.

Wheat

Wheat is Australia's largest crop and is grown in every state in the country. Western Australia is the highest wheat-producing state. Most of Australia's wheat crop is exported to Asia, where the grain is used to make breads and noodles.

wheat

Sugarcane

Sugarcane, a plant from which sugar and syrup are made, requires a lot of water. It is grown on the eastern coasts of Queensland and New South Wales because this region has a lot of rainfall. There are about 4,000 farms that grow sugarcane, and the average sugarcane farm is about 240 acres. About 80% of the crop is exported to other countries.

sugarcane

Cotton

About two-thirds of Australia's cotton is grown in New South Wales. The remaining third is grown in Queensland. Cotton needs even more water than sugarcane does to grow. Cotton is used to make clothing and household items such as sheets and tablecloths. Cotton seeds are also made into cooking oil.

cotton

Wine

Australia is one of the top wine-producing countries in the world. Vineyards are located throughout the country and many different varieties of wine are made. The wine industry in Australia employs about 28,000 people who either grow the grapes or make the wine. Australia exports about 211 million gallons (800 million liters) of wine a year.

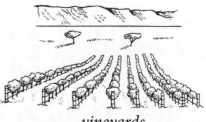

vineyards

Agriculture in Australia

A. Complete each sentence by unscrambling the word or words under the line.
Use the information on the other page to help you.

1. The _____ of Australia do not make good farmland.
   steerds

2. _____ produces more wheat than any other state.
   trenews   silarauta

3. It takes a lot of _____ to grow cotton.
   trewa

4. _____ throughout Australia grow grapes for making wine.
   dravenisy

5. About 4,000 farms in Australia grow _____.
   crungeasa

6. Sugarcane is grown in New South Wales and _____.
   lesquendan

7. Most of Australia's exported wheat goes to _____.
   iasa

8. Most of Australia's cotton crop is grown in _____.
   wen hotsu slewa

B. Wheat and cotton are important crops in Australia. Draw a picture of one thing
that is made from each of these crops. Then label the items.

Wheat	Cotton

Sheep Farming

Although cattle, pigs, poultry, deer, and kangaroos are raised in Australia and New Zealand, sheep are by far the most numerous in the livestock industry. Sheep are raised on large ranches called stations. Sheep provide not only wool, but also meat and dairy products such as cheese.

Fast Facts About the Sheep Industry

- There are about 77 million sheep in Australia. About 75% of Australia's sheep are in New South Wales, Victoria, and Western Australia.

- Australia supplies about 25% of the world's wool, even though it has only about 11% of the world's sheep.

- There are about 45 million sheep in New Zealand. This is about 11 times the number of people in the country! The average size of a flock of sheep is 1,400.

- In the 1990s, there were about twice as many sheep in both Australia and New Zealand as there are today. That number has dropped because more clothing is being made from artificial fabrics such as polyester and acrylic.

- Merino sheep, which are a type of sheep raised in both Australia and New Zealand, have the softest wool. Merino wool is highly valued and is used to make clothing.

- Romney sheep have stronger, coarser wool. The wool from Romney sheep is used for carpets and upholstery. Romney sheep are also raised for their meat. They are valued because they often give birth to twins rather than just one lamb at a time.

- Sheep stations in Australia are huge—often several thousand square miles. It can take hours or even days of travel on rough roads to get to the nearest town. So the stations often have their own stores, schools, and churches for the people who work on them.

- A person who works on a station might be called *Jackaroo* if he is male or *Jillaroo* if she is female.

- Shearing the sheep's wool is done by hand, not machines. Groups of workers travel from station to station to shear sheep. With so many animals to shear, it is important to work quickly. A professional sheep shearer can shear a sheep in less than two minutes and will shear the fleece in one piece. The fastest shearer in the shed is called the *ringer*.

- Sheepdogs play an important role in the sheep farming industry. These intelligent, well-trained dogs help herd the sheep and find strays.

Sheep Farming

A. Circle the correct answer for each clue. Use the information on the other page to help you.

1.	the name for large sheep ranches	**stations**	**rancharoos**
2.	a type of sheep known for its soft wool	**Romney**	**Merino**
3.	the fastest sheep shearer in the shed	**Jackaroo**	**ringer**
4.	an important animal on a sheep station	**sheepdog**	**kangaroo**
5.	the number of sheep in Australia	**45 million**	**77 million**
6.	how sheep are sheared	**by machines**	**by people**
7.	a fabric that does *not* come from sheep's wool	**polyester**	**upholstery**
8.	the average size of a sheep flock in New Zealand	**140**	**1,400**
9.	the percentage of the world's wool supplied by Australia	**55%**	**35%**
10.	a product made from Romney sheep's wool	**carpets**	**sweaters**

B. Imagine that you worked on a sheep station. What do you think you would like about it? What would you dislike? Write a paragraph describing what life on a sheep station might be like for you.

_____

_____

_____

_____

_____

Fishing in Oceania

Fishing is a very important industry for the island nations of Oceania. Many people in this region make their living from fishing. A lot of these people are *subsistence fishermen*. This means that they fish to feed themselves and their families, as well as to sell some of their catch at the local markets.

Other fishermen in Oceania make their living by working on commercial fishing boats. Commercial fishing boats catch huge amounts of fish to sell to other countries. Fishing vessels that enter the waters of Oceania from other parts of the world must pay a fee to the island nations in whose waters they want to fish. The fees are quite large and support a significant part of the islands' economies.

Many different kinds of fish and other marine life are taken from the waters in Oceania. Some of these include snapper, swordfish, grouper, octopus, and lobster. However, the most important commercial fish is tuna. Several types of tuna are caught and processed for export in Oceania, including yellowfin and albacore. In fact, the waters of Oceania produce about 10% of the total tuna fished in the world.

Amount of Fish Caught Yearly in Oceanic Countries

Country	Tons	Metric Tons
Fiji	45,345	41,136
Kiribati	202,732	183,915
Marshall Islands	88,236	80,046
Federated States of Micronesia	189,749	172,137
Nauru	77,036	69,886
Palau	7,285	6,609
Papua New Guinea	682,957	619,568
Samoa	13,673	12,404
Solomon Islands	154,205	139,892
Tonga	8,399	7,619
Tuvalu	40,517	36,756
Vanuatu	40,517	36,756

Food and Agriculture Organization of the United Nations

Fishing in Oceania

A. Fill in the chart with the five countries in Oceania that catch the most fish. Use the chart on the other page to help you.

Rank	Country
1	
2	
3	
4	
5	

B. Answer the questions. Use the information on the other page to help you.

1. Which country catches the least amount of fish? _____

2. Which country catches 12,404 metric tons of fish each year? _____

3. How many tons of fish does Papua New Guinea catch each year? How many metric tons?

   tons: _____   **metric tons:** _____

4. Which two countries catch the same amount of fish per year?

   _____

C. Explain the difference between subsistence fishing and commercial fishing.

_____

_____

_____

Tourism in Oceania

People come from all over the world to visit Australia's Outback, the Great Barrier Reef, and the fjords and glaciers of New Zealand. But tourism is an especially big business for the many small islands of Oceania. Visitors travel to these islands to enjoy beautiful beaches, wild rainforests, and the unique cultures that the islands have to offer. Hotels, restaurants, markets, and activities such as deep-sea fishing, snorkeling, and surfing all bring in money. Many people in Oceania earn a living either as tour guides or by selling native crafts such as baskets, pottery, and jewelry to the tourists. Ecotourism has also become popular. Special eco-tours take people to see secluded, natural places to experience nature without causing harm to the environment.

Some of the most popular tourist destinations in the South Pacific include Fiji, the Cook Islands, Palau, Vanuatu, Tonga, Samoa, and Tahiti.

Fiji

Fiji is often called the "crossroads of the South Pacific" because its location makes it easier to get to than many of the other islands. Several major airlines fly to Fiji, and it is a popular destination for cruise ships as well. People come to Fiji for its many secluded beaches and luxury hotels. Fiji makes more money from tourism than from any other business. In fact, tourism generates about three times as much money as the second-largest industry in the country—sugar production.

Palau

Tourism is the largest industry on the small island nation of Palau. The islands are surrounded by coral reefs and are known for their rich marine life. Most tourists come from Japan and other parts of Asia to scuba dive and snorkel around the reef, where over 1,500 species of fish live. There are also underwater tunnels, caves, and even shipwrecks from World War II to explore. One of the islands in Palau features a body of water called Jellyfish Lake. The lake contains millions of harmless golden jellyfish that swim across it each day, following the sun.

Samoa

The people of Samoa are working to accommodate tourists without damaging the beaches, rainforests, and other natural features of the islands. Samoans do this by offering eco-tours. Tourists usually stay in open-air beach houses called *fales* (FAH-lays) that are run by local villagers instead of staying in a large resort. As a result, visitors learn more about Polynesian culture. They eat local food, shop at local markets, and take tours with guides who have lived on the island their entire lives. These eco-tour programs help local Samoans run their own businesses rather than working for a large resort or tour company.

Tourism in Oceania

Answer each question. Use the information on the other page to help you.

1. Name three ways that Oceania gets money from tourism.

   _____

   _____

   _____

2. Why is Fiji called the "crossroads of the South Pacific"?

   _____

3. Why do most tourists go to Palau?

   _____

   _____

4. Where do people who visit Samoa usually stay and what do they do?

   _____

   _____

   _____

5. If you could visit Fiji, Palau, or Samoa, which would you choose? Why?

   _____

   _____

   _____

Wildlife of Australia and Oceania

Koala

Even though they are often called bears, koalas are actually marsupials.

Habitat
• eucalyptus forests in southwest Australia

Characteristics
• soft gray and white fur
• claws to help climb trees

Diet
• eucalyptus and mistletoe leaves
• bark from 12 kinds of trees

Behavior
• sleeps up to 16 hours a day
• lives in trees
• lives alone rather than in groups

Life Cycle
• mates once a year
• after only 35 days, female gives birth to a baby called a *joey,* which is about the size of a large jelly bean
• joey lives in mother's pouch for about seven months
• can live for up to 17 years

Status
• population has dropped to fewer than 100,000
• threatened by habitat loss; preyed on by wild dogs and fur hunters

Wallaby

There are about 30 different species of wallabies, which are similar to kangaroos.

Habitat
• grassy and rocky areas in Australia and the surrounding islands

Characteristics
• smaller than kangaroo, but can weigh up to 53 pounds (24 kg)
• powerful legs for hopping and kicking
• long tail used for balance

Diet
• leaves and grasses

Behavior
• social animal that lives in a group called a *mob* or *herd*
• nocturnal, or active at night

Life Cycle
• female gives birth to one very small joey that must crawl to the mother's pouch to survive
• joey lives in mother's pouch for several months
• lives about nine years in the wild

Status
• most species are not endangered

The 7 Continents: Australia and Oceania • EMC 3733 • © Evan-Moor Corp.

Wildlife of Australia and Oceania

Tasmanian Devil

This meat-eating marsupial makes a screeching noise when it hunts.

Habitat
• forests of Tasmania

Characteristics
• about as big as a medium-sized dog
• strong, gaping jaws and large teeth that can chew through bone

Diet
• scavenger; eats what other animals have left behind
• will also kill birds and small mammals

Behavior
• nocturnal, or active at night
• roams long distances in search of food
• produces a foul odor when stressed

Life Cycle
• female can give birth to up to 30 tiny joeys at once, but only a few will survive
• joeys stay in mother's pouch for about four months
• lives about eight years in the wild

Status
• endangered species

Platypus

This unusual mammal lays eggs and has a bill like a duck and a tail like a beaver.

Habitat
• lakes, rivers, and streams in eastern Australia

Characteristics
• about the size of a small house cat
• covered in thick brown fur
• male has poisonous stinger on its hind feet

Diet
• insect larvae, worms, and crayfish from the river or lake bottom
• must eat at least one-quarter of its body weight each day

Behavior
• makes burrows in the sides of riverbanks

Life Cycle
• female lays two or three eggs in a burrow
• babies are the size of lima beans and nurse for about four months
• lives about eight years in the wild

Status
• on the list of near-threatened species

Name _____

Wildlife of Australia and Oceania

Kiwi

The kiwi is the national symbol of New Zealand.

Habitat
- scrub forests and grasslands of New Zealand

Characteristics
- about the size of a chicken
- black hair-like feathers
- wings about 1 inch (3 cm) long
- unable to fly

Diet
- grubs, worms, insects, berries, and seeds
- finds food using keen sense of smell

Behavior
- unlike most birds, digs a burrow rather than building a nest

Life Cycle
- female usually lays one large egg
- male sits on the egg for about 80 days
- chicks are born with feathers and look like small adults

Status
- endangered due to dogs, cats, ferrets, and other nonnative animals that eat kiwis and their eggs

Gecko

Geckos are the only reptiles that live on some of the islands of Oceania.

Habitat
- rainforests and deserts throughout Australia and Oceania

Characteristics
- usually under 3 inches (7.5 cm) long
- feet are often leaf-shaped

Diet
- insects
- a few larger species may eat small mammals

Behavior
- makes chirping, squeaking, and barking noises
- can shed tail when attacked and grow another one; the shed tail continues to wriggle after it comes off

Life Cycle
- female usually lays one or two eggs
- New Zealand and New Caledonia species are unusual because they give birth to live young

Status
- most species are not endangered

Wildlife of Australia and Oceania

A. Circle the animal that completes each sentence. Use the information on the other pages to help you.

1. A _____ can shed its tail if it is attacked.

   Tasmanian devil   **platypus**   **gecko**

2. The _____ has babies that are called joeys.

   wallaby   **kiwi**   **gecko**

3. The male _____ has a poisonous stinger on each of its hind feet.

   platypus   **gecko**   **Tasmanian devil**

4. The _____ is native to New Zealand.

   wallaby   **koala**   **kiwi**

5. Although the _____ gives birth to up to 30 babies, only a few will survive.

   Tasmanian devil   **koala**   **platypus**

6. _____ live in eucalyptus forests in Australia.

   Kiwis   **Platypuses**   **Koalas**

7. The _____ must eat one-quarter of its body weight every day.

   platypus   **gecko**   **kiwi**

8. _____ babies look just like small adults.

   Tasmanian devil   **Kiwi**   **Koala**

9. _____ live in groups called mobs or herds.

   Koalas   **Wallabies**   **Platypuses**

B. Which of the six animals would you be most interested in learning more about? Why?

_____

_____

Review

Use words from the box to complete the crossword puzzle.

| coal |
| gold |
| kiwis |
| koalas |
| Manapouri |
| Palau |
| sheep |
| tuna |

Across

3. _____ live in eucalyptus forests in Australia.

5. Some of the world's largest deposits of _____ are in Papua New Guinea.

6. _____ is known for its excellent diving sites.

7. _____ are a kind of bird found only in New Zealand.

Down

1. Australia gets most of its electricity from _____.

2. The _____ power plant is the largest hydropower plant in New Zealand.

4. Several kinds of _____ are caught in the waters of Oceania.

8. There are about 77 million _____ in Australia.

Australian and Oceanic Culture

This section introduces students to the beliefs and traditions of the people of Australia and Oceania. Students learn about cultural activities such as music, art, and sports. They also learn about different types of cuisine and celebrations, as well as religions and native peoples of the continent and surrounding islands.

Each skill in this section is based on the following National Geography Standards:

Essential Element 2: Places and Regions

Standard 6: How culture and experience influence people's perceptions of places and regions

Essential Element 4: Human Systems

Standard 10: The characteristics, distribution, and complexity of Earth's cultural mosaics

CONTENTS

Overview

The culture of a group of people is reflected in its customs, traditions, and beliefs. One way to learn about a particular culture is to explore its history, celebrations, art, and literature. There are literally thousands of different cultures within Australia and Oceania, each with its own set of customs and beliefs.

Tourist Attractions

Tourists who visit Australia and Oceania can see a wide range of unique sights. One of the most recognized landmarks in the world is Australia's Sydney Opera House, where over 3,000 performances are held every year. In New Zealand, people visit the Waitangi Treaty Grounds to learn more about the country's history. And in the Federated States of Micronesia, a main attraction is the ruins of the city of Nan Madol.

Native Cultures, Arts, and Entertainment

Australia and Oceania have many different native cultures. The Aboriginal people have lived in Australia for thousands of years, long before Europeans arrived. In New Zealand, the native people are called Maori (MOW-ree), and they live by a set of rules to control behavior and beliefs. The native cultures of the islands of Oceania place importance on *kinship,* or family relationships. All of these cultures are known for their artwork, including paintings, carvings, and even body tattoos.

Sports are an important form of entertainment to the people of Australia and Oceania. Surfing, sailing, and Australian Rules Football are some favorites.

Religions

Although over half of the people in Australia and Oceania are Christian, many other religions are also practiced. Islam is one of the fastest growing religions in Australia. There are also small populations of Hindus, Buddhists, and Jews. In Oceania, many cultures have mixed their traditional beliefs with Christianity.

Cuisine

Most Australians eat a great deal of meat, especially beef. Traditional Australian dishes include meat pies, a simple bread called *damper,* and Vegemite, which is a sandwich spread. In Oceania, seafood is an important source of protein. People also eat starchy vegetables, such as sweet potatoes, cassavas, taro root, and yams.

Celebrations

New Year's Day is a big celebration in Australia and parts of Oceania because of the time zone in which they are located. They are the first countries to celebrate the holiday each year. Australians also observe Australia Day, a day of national pride. On Papua New Guinea, people celebrate Hiri Moale to commemorate a historic annual voyage.

Overview

Fill in the bubble to answer each question.

1. Where are the Nan Madol ruins located?

   Ⓐ Sydney

   Ⓑ New Zealand

   Ⓒ Micronesia

   Ⓓ Papua New Guinea

2. Which of these foods is a popular sandwich spread in Australia?

   Ⓐ cassava

   Ⓑ taro root

   Ⓒ Vegemite

   Ⓓ damper

3. In what country is Hiri Moale celebrated?

   Ⓐ Australia

   Ⓑ New Zealand

   Ⓒ Fiji

   Ⓓ Papua New Guinea

4. What are the native people of New Zealand called?

   Ⓐ Maori

   Ⓑ Waitangi

   Ⓒ Aboriginals

   Ⓓ Madol

5. Which of these is one of the fastest growing religions in Australia?

   Ⓐ Judaism

   Ⓑ Islam

   Ⓒ Hinduism

   Ⓓ Christianity

Australia and Oceania's Tourist Attractions

Sydney Opera House

With its uniquely shaped roofs, the Sydney Opera House is one of the most familiar landmarks in the world. It was designed by Danish architect Jorn Utzon and was completed in 1973. The Opera House is not just one building, but a complex of different structures. It has over 1,000 rooms and holds 3,000 events each year. Over 2 million people a year attend performances, and another 200,000 people come for tours of the building.

Waitangi Treaty Grounds

The Waitangi Treaty Grounds are located on the northern end of the North Island of New Zealand. The grounds are the site where the first treaty between the British government and the native Maori people was signed on February 6, 1840. This agreement was an important step toward resolving the conflicts between British colonists and the Maori. People come to the Waitangi Treaty Grounds to tour the Treaty House, which is one of New Zealand's oldest homes, and the *Te Whare Runanga,* which is a Maori meeting house. This building features carvings representing all of the Maori tribes in New Zealand. Another attraction is the 118 foot (36 m) Maori canoe that is launched every February 6 to celebrate the treaty signing. This huge canoe is 70 years old and requires 80 paddlers to move it.

ceremonial waka taua, *or war canoe, at the Waitangi Treaty Grounds*

Nan Madol

Nan Madol are the ruins of an ancient city off the eastern coast of Pohnpei Island in the Federated States of Micronesia. Built in the 12th century, the city is believed to have housed royalty. The ruins are considered remarkable because the entire city was built on more than 100 stone platforms that were constructed over the coral reefs surrounding the island. There are many different structures, including stone buildings, kitchens, and tombs. No one knows how this huge amount of stone was transported from the main island to the reefs.

Australia and Oceania's Tourist Attractions

A. Complete each sentence by unscrambling the word or words under the line. Use the information on the other page to help you.

1. Architect _____ designed the Sydney Opera House.
   rojn zutno

2. People believe that _____ lived in Nan Madol.
   lotyary

3. The Sydney Opera House has over 1,000 _____.
   omors

4. Nan Madol was constructed from stones laid over _____.
   locra sfere

5. The Waitangi Treaty Grounds are located in _____.
   wen naledza

6. The Maori meeting house at Waitangi features many _____.
   vignarcs

7. Nan Madol is located off the eastern coast of _____.
   heppino

8. A large Maori _____ is launched every February 6.
   neaco

9. The roofs of the Sydney Opera House are very _____.
   qunuei

10. The British and the Maori signed a _____ in 1840.
    rattey

B. Which of the three places on the other page would you like to visit the most? Explain your answer.

_____

_____

_____

Arts and Entertainment

Throughout history, the peoples of Australia and Oceania have used natural materials from their environment to create pictures and designs. Although many of these artifacts are thousands of years old, contemporary artists are still inspired by their designs.

Aboriginal Paintings

The Aborigines are Australia's original inhabitants. They have been making paintings on rocks and tree bark for thousands of years. The oldest surviving paintings were made about 30,000 years ago on rock walls in central Australia. Aboriginal art often tells the story of *Dreamtime*—a period when, according to Aboriginal myth, everything was created. Aboriginal art often features animals, animal tracks, and humans, as well as geometrical shapes such as circles and diamonds. One common artistic style is called *dot art,* where pictures are made using many small dots. Today, many artists continue to create traditional Aboriginal art.

Maori Carvings

The Maori, the native people of New Zealand, are known for their beautiful wood, stone, and bone carvings. Most wood-carvings are done on buildings or canoes. Older Maori carvings are of people who are thought to be important ancestors. There are also carvings of mermaid-like creatures, beings that look like a mix between birds and humans, and animals such as lizards, birds, whales, and fish. Traditionally, the carving is done with an *adze,* an axe-like tool. The craft of carving is passed down within Maori families. Many of today's carvers are the descendents of families who have been carving for thousands of years.

Polynesian Tattoos

For thousands of years, people across Oceania have decorated their bodies with tattoos. In fact, before European missionaries forbade the practice in the 1800s, almost every adult in Polynesia had tattoos. Getting tattooed was a sacred event, and tattoos were done by respected shamans. The shaman used needles made from bone or tortoise shell. The needles were dipped in soot mixed with oil. Then they were tapped into the skin with a small hammer. The designs had personal meaning, depicting status, family, activities, and achievements. Today, many modern Polynesians still get traditional tattoos.

Name _____

Arts and Entertainment

A. Next to each term, write the letter of the clue that describes it. Use the information on the other page to help you.

_____ 1. Aborigines

_____ 2. Dreamtime

_____ 3. dot art

_____ 4. Maori

_____ 5. adze

_____ 6. tortoise shell

_____ 7. tattoos

_____ 8. missionaries

a. a material used to make needles for tattooing

b. the native people of Australia

c. a Maori carving tool

d. people who outlawed tribal tattoos in Oceania

e. the time of creation in Aboriginal myth

f. a type of body art in Oceania

g. the native people of New Zealand

h. a style of Aboriginal painting

B. Color the Aboriginal picture. Then write a caption about it.

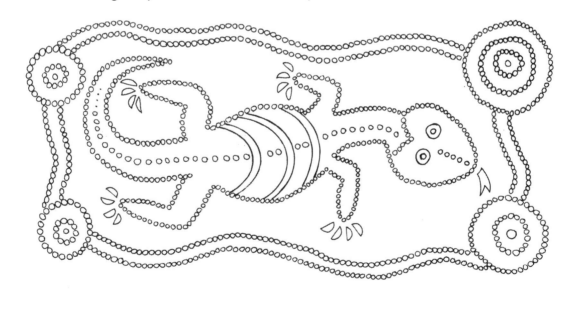

_____

_____

_____

Arts and Entertainment

Movie Industry

Many movies and some TV shows have been filmed in the Australia/Oceania region. New Zealand, with its rugged landscape, is an especially popular filming location.

Movie or TV Show	Location(s)	Fun Facts
The Chronicles of Narnia (2005, 2008, 2010)	New Zealand, Australia	Andrew Adamson, the director of the first two movies of the series, is from New Zealand. He said, "New Zealand gave us the magic of Narnia."
Survivor (2000–2010)	Australia, Palau, Cook Islands, Fiji, F. Polynesia, Samoa, Micronesia, Vanuatu	Nine seasons of this popular reality TV show were filmed in remote areas of Australia and Oceania. The producers included parts of the native cultures in the music, set decorations, tribe names, and challenges.
Bridge to Terabithia (2007)	New Zealand	Because New Zealand has no squirrels, the squirrels shown in the movie were either added digitally, or the scenes were filmed elsewhere and added to the film.
The Lord of the Rings Trilogy (2001, 2002, 2003)	New Zealand	The three *Lord of the Rings* movies were the biggest production in New Zealand and one of the biggest ever in the world. It added about 200 million dollars to the New Zealand economy.
Whale Rider (2002)	New Zealand	Keisha Castle-Hughes, the Maori girl who starred in this film about a girl fighting to fulfill her destiny, had to do many things that females in Maori culture are not supposed to do. The crew performed special chants to ward off bad luck.
Cast Away (2000)	Fiji	More than an hour of this movie, starring Tom Hanks, was shot on or near the beach. The sound had to be redone because the noise of the waves made it impossible to hear the actor's words.

Circle the movies or shows in the chart that you have seen. Then answer the questions.

1. How did *The Lord of the Rings* trilogy help New Zealand?

   _____

2. In what ways did *Survivor* include local cultures?

   _____

3. What interesting fact about New Zealand affected the filming of *Bridge to Terabithia*?

   _____

Arts and Entertainment

Music

The song "Waltzing Matilda" is often said to be the unofficial national anthem of Australia. The song contains a lot of colorful slang (informal words), which Australia is well-known for. *Matilda* is slang for a "camping backpack" and *Waltzing Matilda* means "walking with a backpack."

Use the glossary at the bottom of this page to tell what the verses in "Waltzing Matilda" mean. Try to summarize each verse rather than translating it word for word.

"Waltzing Matilda" Verses	What They Mean
Once a jolly swagman sat beside the billabong, Under the shade of a coolabah tree, And he sang as he sat and waited till his billy boiled, "You'll come a-waltzing, Matilda with me." Chorus: Waltzing Matilda, Waltzing Matilda, You'll come a-waltzing, Matilda with me.	
Down came a jumbuck to drink at that billabong, Up jumped the swagman and grabbed him with glee, And he sang as he shoved that jumbuck in his tucker bag, "You'll come a-waltzing, Matilda with me." (Chorus)	
Up rode the squatter, mounted on his thoroughbred, Down came the troopers, one, two, three, "Where's that jolly jumbuck you've got in your tucker bag?" "You'll come a-waltzing, Matilda with me." (Chorus)	
Up jumped the swagman and sprang into the billabong, "You'll never catch me alive," cried he. And his ghost may be heard as you pass by that billabong, "You'll come a-waltzing, Matilda with me." (Chorus)	

Glossary

billabong: a water hole

billy: a small kettle used to boil water for tea

coolabah tree: a type of eucalyptus tree

jumbuck: sheep

squatter: landowner

swagman: traveler or hobo

trooper: police officer

tucker bag: a bag for storing food

Arts and Entertainment

Sports

Both competitive and recreational sports play a big role in the lives of Australians, New Zealanders, and South Pacific islanders. Watersports are particularly popular in this ocean-based culture.

Watersports

The dramatic surf and beautiful beaches of Australia provide many ideal places for swimming and surfing. Some of the best professional surfers in the world, in fact, are from Australia. Surfing is also very popular on New Zealand and the islands of Fiji, Tonga, and Tahiti.

Another popular sport is sailing. People come from all over the world to sail around the islands of the Pacific. Many people sail for fun, but others compete in major sailing competitions, such as the Sailing World Cup. Australia has won the Sailing World Cup 12 times, more than any other country.

The South Pacific Games

The South Pacific Games are a multi-sport event that takes place once every four years to promote goodwill and kinship among the island nations of Oceania. The event lasts for two weeks and is held at a different location each time. The first South Pacific Games were held in Fiji in 1963. The games were attended by 8,000 spectators, and 770 athletes competed.

Today, about 5,000 athletes compete in 33 different sports at the games. Some of these sports include basketball, beach volleyball, soccer, rugby, badminton, sailing, cricket, karate, and archery.

Australian Rules Football

Australian Rules Football is by far the most popular winter sport in Australia, as well as in many parts of Oceania. Australian Rules Football is somewhat similar to rugby, although the field is oval-shaped rather than rectangular. The players wear no protective gear and are allowed to tackle their opponents.

The first Australian Rules Football league was formed in the state of Victoria in 1859. At that time there were eight teams. Today, there are 16 professional teams. Professional games draw thousands of spectators who enthusiastically cheer for their teams.

Arts and Entertainment

Sports

A. Read each statement. Circle **yes** if it is true or **no** if it is false. Use the information on the other page to help you.

1.	There are few places to go surfing in Australia.	Yes	No
2.	Australian Rules Football is played on an oval-shaped field.	Yes	No
3.	Australia has won 16 Sailing World Cups.	Yes	No
4.	Some of the best surfers in the world are from Australia.	Yes	No
5.	The South Pacific Games are held every year.	Yes	No
6.	Australian Rules Football started in New South Wales.	Yes	No
7.	About 5,000 athletes participate in the South Pacific Games.	Yes	No
8.	Tahiti is not a good place to go surfing.	Yes	No
9.	The first South Pacific Games were held in Fiji.	Yes	No
10.	Players do not wear protective gear in Australian Rules Football.	Yes	No
11.	Cricket, volleyball, and rugby are played in the South Pacific Games.	Yes	No
12.	Cricket is the most popular sport in Australia.	Yes	No

B. If you were going to live in Australia for a year, which sport would you want to try—surfing, sailing, or Australian Rules Football? Explain your answer.

_____

_____

_____

Major Religions of Australia and Oceania

Oceania

Before the Europeans came to the islands of Oceania, the native people followed many different traditional religions. Most of these religions practiced the worship of many gods. Some cultures had a god named Tangaroa, who was the god of the sea. Other island religions believed in the Adaro, who were evil sea spirits. Many of the traditional religions had beliefs about the spirits of dead ancestors, as well as myths about how the world was made.

By the late 1800s, most of the island people had been converted to Christianity by missionaries. On some islands, the traditional practices were forbidden, while on others, old traditions were combined with Christianity. In some places, especially in Melanesia, traditions involving food, music, and ceremonies are still practiced, and most islanders still have ways of honoring their ancestors.

Australia

Just as in Oceania, missionaries came to Australia and converted most of the native people to Christianity. Today, just over 60% of the population identify themselves as Christian. However, most of these people do not consider themselves to be religious and do not attend church regularly.

The fastest growing religions in Australia are Buddhism and Islam. This is because of the large numbers of immigrants from Asia and the Middle East who come to Australia. There are also small groups of Jews and Hindus. And a small percentage of Aboriginal people are still deeply devoted to their traditional religious practices.

The pie chart below shows how Australians responded when asked what religion, if any, they practiced.

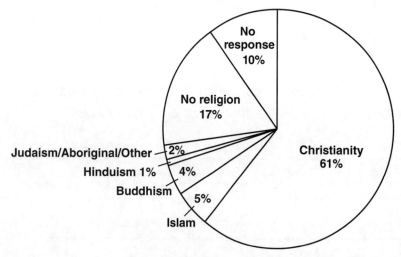

State Government of Victoria, Australia, Dept. of Human Services

Major Religions of Australia and Oceania

A. Circle the correct answer to complete each sentence. Use information on the other page to help you.

1. The fastest growing religions in Australia are Buddhism and _____.

   Christianity   **Islam**   **Hinduism**

2. Tangaroa is the name of a _____.

   god   **spirit**   **religion**

3. About 6% of the population of Australia practice Islam and _____.

   Hinduism   **Buddhism**   **Judaism**

4. On some islands in Oceania, native religions were mixed with _____.

   Islam   **Hinduism**   **Christianity**

5. About _____% of Australians do not have a religion.

   61   **17**   **27**

6. By the late _____, most of the people in Oceania had converted to Christianity.

   1600s   **1700s**   **1800s**

B. Use the information on the other page to answer the questions.

1. What is one way that native people still practice their traditional religions in Oceania?

   _____

2. Why are Buddhism and Islam growing in Australia?

   _____

   _____

Native Cultures of Australia and Oceania

Aborigines

The Aborigines are the native people of Australia. For over 40,000 years before the Europeans came to Australia, the Aboriginal people lived in *nomadic,* or traveling, hunter–gatherer clans. Surviving in the Outback was not easy, and most of their time was spent obtaining food and water. Because they moved frequently, the Aborigines had few possessions. They also had no concept of land ownership. They believed that they, like the plants and animals, belonged to the land. Religious beliefs centered on Dreamtime, the mythical time when ancestor spirits moved across the land and gave it form. Stories of Dreamtime were told in art and song.

Today, most Aborigines live in cities or work as stockmen, or people who look after livestock, on Outback stations. However, a small number still live much as their ancestors in the Outback did for thousands of years.

The Maori

It is thought that the Maori came to New Zealand around AD 1300 from islands in Micronesia. According to Maori legend, they traveled thousands of miles across the ocean in several large canoes. Many modern-day Maori can trace their ancestry back to one of these canoes. Traditionally, the Maori lived by a set of strict rules called *tapu* that governed behavior and beliefs. Breaking the tapu was thought to bring serious consequences from the gods.

Today, many parts of the Maori culture continue to thrive, and Maori children still learn the native language, traditional songs, and stories.

Island Cultures

Many people on the islands of Oceania live in small villages where family relationships, or kinships, are very important. These kinships determine how people are treated and how they behave. People help family members—even distant relatives—in times of need. In return, people know that should they be in need, their family members will be there to help.

Many island families still pay *bridewealth* when there is a marriage. This is a payment of goods from the groom's family to the bride's. Because the bride goes to live with the groom's family, the payment is thought to make up for the loss of her labor and company. It is also a way for the groom's family to show that they value the bride and will treat her well.

Native Cultures of Australia and Oceania

Use the information on the other page to answer the questions.

1. Why did the Aborigines in the Outback have few possessions?

_____

2. What is *tapu*?

_____

3. What is Dreamtime?

_____

_____

4. How do people in island cultures show that their kinships are important?

_____

_____

5. According to Maori myth, how did the Maori come to New Zealand?

_____

6. How did Aboriginal people spend most of their time?

_____

7. What are two reasons that a groom's family in Oceania might pay bridewealth?

_____

_____

_____

Australian and Oceanic Cuisine

Australian Cuisine

When settlers came to Australia from Great Britain, they brought their food traditions with them. Many of those dishes, such as meat pies, sausage rolls, and meat stews, are still popular today. Cooking styles from other European and Asian countries have influenced Australian cuisine as well.

Meat makes up a large portion of the Australian diet. Australians are famous for holding barbeques (often called "barbies") where they grill beef, chicken, pork, shrimp, and other seafood. In addition, Australians might eat unusual meats such as crocodile, emu, kangaroo, and wombat. At one time, the animals were eaten mostly by people living in the Outback. In recent years, however, these meats have shown up on the menus of some of Australia's finest restaurants.

Some foods are unique to Australia. A simple bread called *damper* is frequently eaten in the Outback. It is traditionally cooked over an open fire. For dessert, *Pavlova* is often served. Pavlova is made of egg whites that have been whipped and baked. The outside gets crisp and the inside is soft and sticky. The dessert is topped with fruit and whipped cream. Another popular dessert is called Lamingtons, which are sponge cake cubes dipped in chocolate and rolled in coconut. But perhaps Australia's best-known food is Vegemite, a salty brown spread made from yeast extract that is used in sandwiches and on toast.

Oceanic Cuisine

Seafood is the main source of protein for many people in Oceania. In addition to fish, people eat sea turtles, lobsters, crabs, oysters, and other shellfish. Starchy vegetables are another important part of the island diet. These include breadfruit, taro root, sweet potatoes, yams, and cassavas. People also eat coconuts and many kinds of fruit that grow on the islands. Bananas, mangos, papayas, and several kinds of citrus fruit are eaten throughout the day or added to the main meal.

Eating together is an important part of island culture in Oceania. It is believed to strengthen family and community ties, as well as the status and role of each person. Large feasts are featured in many cultural celebrations on the islands. An essential part of the feast is the giving away of food. Wealthy people give away large quantities of food in order to display their generosity. A pig and other traditional foods are often baked in an underground pit lined with hot stones. During the many hours it takes to cook the food, there are storytelling, games, singing, and dancing. The guests are served in order of their importance.

Australian and Oceanic Cuisine

A. Write the Australian and Oceanic foods in the correct category. Use the word box below and the information on the other page to help you.

Pavlova	emu	cassava	Lamingtons	wombat	Vegemite
damper	yam	lobster	breadfruit	papaya	taro root

Meat or Seafood	Vegetable or Fruit	Dessert	Other

B. Answer the questions.

1. Which food described on the other page would you most like to try? Why?

    _____

    _____

2. Which food would you least like to try? Why?

    _____

    _____

Celebrations of Australia and Oceania

New Year's Day

Because of the time zone in which they are located, Australia and some islands in Oceania are the first countries to celebrate New Year's Day each January 1. Millennium Island in the nation of Kiribati is the first landmass on Earth to see the new year. New Zealand, Tonga, and Fiji are close behind.

Celebrations include parties, dancing, and fireworks. Sydney, Australia, has one of the world's largest fireworks displays. The fireworks are held over the Sydney Harbour Bridge and over 1 million people gather to watch them. Millions more watch them on television around the world.

Australia Day

On January 26, 1788, Captain Arthur Phillip raised the British flag at Sydney Cove and claimed New South Wales for Britain. Australia Day, which was first called Founder's Day, began as a celebration of this event. Today, Australia Day is a national holiday that is celebrated throughout the continent. It is a time for Australians to show pride in their country. It is also a time for people to recognize and honor the place that the Aborigines hold in the country's history. Formal ceremonies to honor the Aboriginal people are part of some celebrations. There are other formal events, including flag raisings, citizenship ceremonies, and community awards. Fun activities include picnics, parades, performances, games, and fireworks.

Hiri Moale

Hiri Moale is celebrated every September 16 in Papua New Guinea. It is a time to commemorate the ancient trade voyages of the native Motu people, who lived in the area now called Port Moresby. Each year, the Motu sailed off to trade their clay pots for *sago,* a starchy food that comes from the sago palm plant. Up to 20 large canoes were built for the voyage. The canoes were crewed by about 600 men and carried about 20,000 clay pots on each journey.

The canoes sailed west to the Gulf of Papua. Although the trip took only about a week, the sailors had to stay on shore for at least 50 days to wait for the seasons to change and bring winds that would carry them home. The trip home took much longer and was much more dangerous because the new season produced storms and heavy seas. When the sailors arrived home safely with their cargo, there was a huge feast and celebration. In fact, Hiri Moale means "happy return of voyage." The last of these trading voyages took place in the 1950s. Today, the holiday is celebrated with canoe races, singing, musical competitions, and feasts.

Celebrations of Australia and Oceania

Read each clue below and write the correct word or words on the numbered lines.
Then use the numbers to crack the code!

1. What is the first country in the world to see the new year every January 1?

   $\overline{}\ \overline{}\ \overline{}\ \overline{}\ \overline{}\ \overline{}\ \overline{}\ \overline{}$
   8   10   1   10   17   18   25   10

2. Each year, the Motu people made thousands of ____ to trade for food.

   $\overline{}\ \overline{}\ \overline{}\ \overline{}\qquad \overline{}\ \overline{}\ \overline{}\ \overline{}$
   16   7   18   20   3   4   25   26

3. On Australia Day, there are ____ ceremonies to honor the Aboriginal people.

   $\overline{}\ \overline{}\ \overline{}\ \overline{}\ \overline{}\ \overline{}$
   13   4   1   6   18   7

4. What Australian city holds one of the largest fireworks displays in the world?

   $\overline{}\ \overline{}\ \overline{}\ \overline{}\ \overline{}\ \overline{}$
   26   20   15   5   14   20

5. The Motu traveled to the Gulf of Papua in large ____.

   $\overline{}\ \overline{}\ \overline{}\ \overline{}\ \overline{}\ \overline{}$
   16   18   5   4   14   26

6. Australia Day is celebrated on ____ 26 each year.

   $\overline{}\ \overline{}\ \overline{}\ \overline{}\ \overline{}\ \overline{}\ \overline{}$
   9   18   5   24   18   1   20

Crack the Code!

The Motu made sails for their canoes using ____, or leaves.

$\overline{}\ \overline{}\ \overline{}\ \overline{}\qquad \overline{}\ \overline{}\ \overline{}\ \overline{}\ \overline{}\ \overline{}$
3   18   7   6   13   1   4   5   15   26

Review

Use words from the box to complete the crossword puzzle.

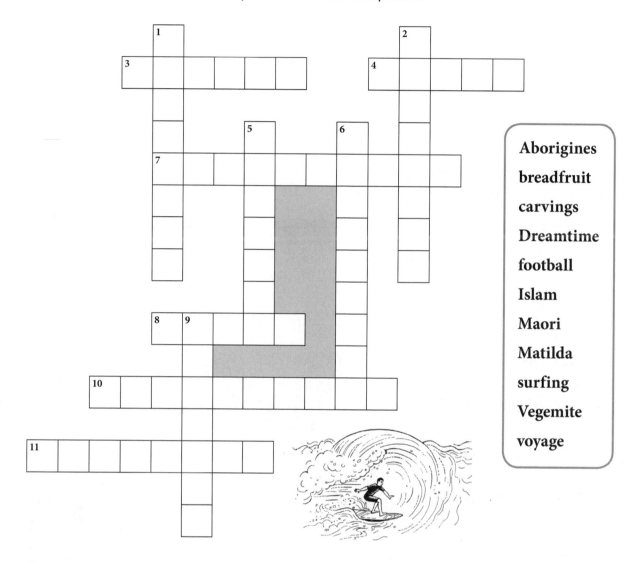

Aborigines

breadfruit

carvings

Dreamtime

football

Islam

Maori

Matilda

surfing

Vegemite

voyage

Across

3. Hiri Moale celebrates the return from a _____.
4. the native people of New Zealand
7. a starchy vegetable of Oceania
8. a fast-growing religion in Australia
10. the native people of Australia
11. a popular Australian bread spread

Down

1. Australia has its own form of _____.
2. The Maori are known for their wood _____.
5. "Waltzing _____" is the unofficial national anthem of Australia.
6. a time when everything was created, according to Aboriginal myths
9. a popular watersport in Australia

Assessment

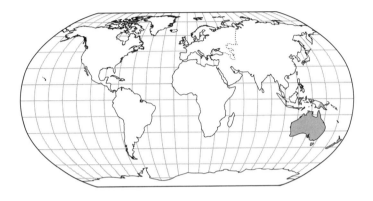

This section of Australia and Oceania provides two cumulative assessments that you can use to evaluate students' acquisition of the information presented in this book. The first assessment requires students to identify selected cities, countries, landforms, and bodies of water on a combined physical and political map. The second assessment is a two-page multiple-choice test covering information from all sections of the book. Use one or both assessments as culminating activities for your class's study of Australia and Oceania.

CONTENTS

Map Test

Write the name of the country, city, landform, or body of water that matches each number. Use the words in the box to help you.

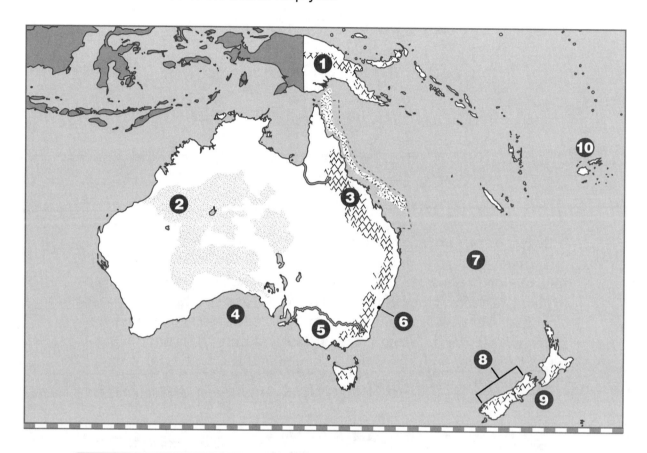

Great Australian Bight	Papua New Guinea	Southern Alps	Fiji
Great Dividing Range	New Zealand	Murray River	
Great Sandy Desert	Pacific Ocean	Sydney	

1. _____   6. _____

2. _____   7. _____

3. _____   8. _____

4. _____   9. _____

5. _____   10. _____

Multiple-Choice Test

Fill in the bubble to answer each question or complete each sentence.

1. Australia is the ⎯⎯ continent.
   - Ⓐ largest
   - Ⓑ second-largest
   - Ⓒ third-largest
   - Ⓓ smallest

2. Which ocean is east of Australia?
   - Ⓐ Pacific
   - Ⓑ Arctic
   - Ⓒ Atlantic
   - Ⓓ Indian

3. In which two hemispheres is Australia located?
   - Ⓐ Northern and Eastern
   - Ⓑ Southern and Western
   - Ⓒ Southern and Eastern
   - Ⓓ Northern and Western

4. Which of these is *not* a country in Oceania?
   - Ⓐ Fiji
   - Ⓑ Australia
   - Ⓒ Papua New Guinea
   - Ⓓ Tuvalu

5. Which of these is the tallest mountain in Oceania?
   - Ⓐ Mount Kosciuszko
   - Ⓑ Mount Cook
   - Ⓒ Mount Wilhelm
   - Ⓓ Mount Everest

6. What is the term for a ring of small coral islands?
   - Ⓐ lagoon
   - Ⓑ islet
   - Ⓒ fjord
   - Ⓓ atoll

7. Which of these is *not* the name of a desert in Australia?
   - Ⓐ Uluru Desert
   - Ⓑ Gibson Desert
   - Ⓒ Great Victoria Desert
   - Ⓓ Great Sandy Desert

8. Which of these is the longest river in Australia?
   - Ⓐ Darling
   - Ⓑ Murray
   - Ⓒ Murrumbidgee
   - Ⓓ Amazon

Multiple-Choice Test

9. Where is the Manapouri Hydropower station located?

Ⓐ Australia

Ⓑ New Zealand

Ⓒ Kiribati

Ⓓ Samoa

10. What is a large sheep farm in Australia called?

Ⓐ station

Ⓑ ranch

Ⓒ farmie

Ⓓ jumbuck

11. Which country in Oceania is often called the "crossroads of the South Pacific"?

Ⓐ Marshall Islands

Ⓑ Palau

Ⓒ Fiji

Ⓓ Samoa

12. Which of these animals is *not* a marsupial?

Ⓐ wallaby

Ⓑ kiwi

Ⓒ Tasmanian devil

Ⓓ koala

13. What is Dreamtime?

Ⓐ a style of Aboriginal painting

Ⓑ a mythical time of creation

Ⓒ a welcoming ceremony

Ⓓ a type of Maori carving

14. Which film trilogy was shot in New Zealand?

Ⓐ *Cast Away*

Ⓑ *Bridge to Terabithia*

Ⓒ *The Lord of the Rings*

Ⓓ *Whale Rider*

15. Which of these is *not* a starchy vegetable eaten in Oceania?

Ⓐ yam

Ⓑ taro root

Ⓒ cassava

Ⓓ mango

16. What is the name of the festival that celebrates a "happy return of voyage"?

Ⓐ Hiri Moale

Ⓑ Australia Day

Ⓒ New Year's Day

Ⓓ Waltzing Matilda

Note Takers

This section provides four note taker forms that give students the opportunity to culminate their study of Australia and Oceania by doing independent research on places or animals of their choice. (Some suggested topics are given below.) Students may use printed reference materials or Internet sites to gather information on their topics. A cover page is also provided so that students may create a booklet of note takers and any other reproducible pages from the book that you would like students to save.

FORMS

Select a physical feature of Australia and Oceania. Write notes about it to complete each section.

_____

(Name of Physical Feature)

N
W   E
S

Location

_____

_____

_____

Interesting Facts

_____

_____

_____

_____

_____

_____

_____

_____

_____

_____

Description

_____

_____

_____

_____

_____

_____

_____

_____

_____

Animals or Plants

_____

_____

_____

Draw an Australian or Oceanic animal. Write notes about it to complete each section.

_____

(Name of Animal)

Habitat

_____
_____
_____
_____

Endangered? (Yes) (No)

Physical Characteristics

_____
_____
_____
_____

Diet

_____
_____
_____

Behaviors

_____
_____
_____

Enemies/Defenses

_____
_____
_____

Name _____

Draw an Australian or Oceanic tourist attraction. Then write notes about it to complete each section.

_____
(Name of Tourist Attraction)

Location

N
W E
S

_____
_____
_____
_____

Description

_____
_____
_____
_____
_____
_____
_____
_____
_____
_____

Interesting Facts

_____
_____
_____
_____

Name _____

Select an Australian or Oceanic city you would like to visit. Write notes about it to complete each section.

My Trip to _____
(Name of City)

N
W E
S

Location

_____

_____

_____

_____

How I Would Get There

_____

_____

_____

_____

Things I Would See and Do

_____

_____

_____

_____

_____

_____

_____

Foods I Would Eat

_____

_____

_____

_____

Learning the Language

How to Say "Hello"

_____

How to Say "Goodbye"

_____

AUSTRALIA

Page 5

1. D   2. A   3. B   4. D   5. A

Page 6

A. Africa, Antarctica, west, Indian, east, Oceania, Pacific

B. Students should color Africa orange and Antarctica gray, circle the Pacific Ocean in blue, and draw a panda on Asia.

Page 9

A. 1. c   2. f   3. h   4. e   5. d   6. b   7. g   8. i   9. a
B.

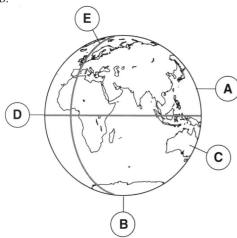

Page 11

A.
1. equator	6. latitude lines
2. prime meridian	7. 15 degrees
3. south	8. parallels
4. 120°E	9. 15°S
5. 30°S	10. 150°E

B. Most of Australia and Oceania are located south of the equator and east of the prime meridian, so the latitude and longitude lines used to find their absolute locations are labeled in degrees south and east.

Page 12

1. No	6. Yes
2. Yes	7. No
3. Yes	8. Yes
4. No	9. Yes
5. Yes	10. Yes

Page 14

Across	**Down**
1. hemispheres	2. smallest
3. Africa	3. absolute
6. equator	4. islands
7. Pacific	5. projection

Page 17

1. C   2. C   3. A   4. B   5. D

Page 18

A.

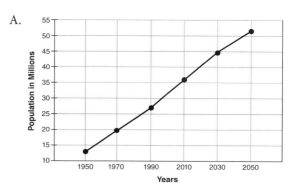

B. Answers will vary—e.g.,
1. About how many people lived in Australia and Oceania in 1990? Answer: About 27 million.
2. In what year will there be more than 50 million people in Australia and Oceania? Answer: 2050.

Page 19

C.
1. tripled	5. 35
2. at about the same rate	6. 45
3. 13	7. four
4. 7	8. 1990

Page 20

B. 1. Micronesia
2. Australia
3. Answers will vary—e.g.,
   Marshall Islands, Solomon Islands, and the Federated States of Micronesia

Page 21

A. Students should circle the names of the countries in the following colors:

Green: Australia

Orange: Fiji, Papua New Guinea, Solomon Islands, Vanuatu

Red: Kiribati, Marshall Islands, Federated States of Micronesia, Nauru, Palau

Yellow: New Zealand, Samoa, Tonga, Tuvalu

Page 22

A. 1. Australia is the largest country in Australia and Oceania.
   2. New Zealand is 104,454 square miles in size.
   3. The Solomon Islands are the fourth-largest country in Australia and Oceania.

Page 23

B. Students should color Australia, Papua New Guinea, and New Zealand different colors. They should also trace the dotted lines around the Solomon Islands and Fiji in different colors. Then they should complete the map key.

Five Largest Countries	Color
1. Australia	1. Color will vary.
2. Papua New Guinea	2. Color will vary.
3. New Zealand	3. Color will vary.
4. Solomon Islands	4. Color will vary.
5. Fiji	5. Color will vary.

Page 24

A. 1. The Marshall Islands are the third-smallest country in Oceania.
   2. The smallest country in Oceania is just 21 square kilometers large.
   3. The fourth-smallest country, Palau, is located in Micronesia.

B. Students should trace the dotted lines around Nauru, Tuvalu, Marshall Islands, Palau, and the Federated States of Micronesia in different colors. Then they should complete the map key.

Page 25

Five Smallest Countries	Color
1. Nauru	1. Color will vary.
2. Tuvalu	2. Color will vary.
3. Marshall Islands	3. Color will vary.
4. Palau	4. Color will vary.
5. Federated States of Micronesia	5. Color will vary.

Page 26

A. 1. d   6. g
   2. f   7. h
   3. j   8. b
   4. c   9. a
   5. i   10. e

B. 1. 3
   2. 5
   3. Samoa and Vanuatu

Page 27

C. Answers will vary—e.g.,
   1. There are 10 countries in Australia and Oceania with a population of more than 100,000.
   2. Four of the 10 most populated countries are located in Melanesia.
   3. Fiji has just under 1 million people living there.

Page 29

A. 1. Midway Island   6. Wake Island
   2. Cook Islands   7. Guam
   3. New Caledonia   8. United States
   4. Pitcairn Islands Group   9. 291,000
   5. kilometers

B. 1. 3
   2. 7
   3. Norfolk Island
   4. Polynesia
   5. Cook Islands, Niue Island, Tokelau

Page 30

A. 1. No   6. Yes
   2. No   7. Yes
   3. Yes   8. No
   4. No   9. Yes
   5. No   10. Yes

Page 31

B. Students should color Western Australia, Northern Territory, South Australia, Queensland, New South Wales, Australian Capital Territory, Victoria, and Tasmania different colors. Then they should write a caption.

Captions will vary—e.g., Australia is divided into six states and two territories.

Page 32

A. 1. Papua New Guinea
   2. Vanuatu
   3. Fiji
   4. Solomon Islands
   5. Norfolk Island
   6. Vanua Levu, Viti Levu

B. Students should circle Fiji, Papua New Guinea, Solomon Islands, and Vanuatu in green and New Caledonia and Norfolk Island in red.

Page 34

Rank	Country	Population
1	Kiribati	113,000
2	Federated States of Micronesia	107,000
3	Marshall Islands	65,000
4	Palau	21,000
5	Nauru	14,000

1. 99,000
2. Kiribati and Federated States of Micronesia

Page 36

A. 1. Samoa
   2. Tokelau
   3. Tonga
   4. Tuvalu
   5. New Zealand
   6. Polynesia
   7. south
   8. Midway Island

B. Students should circle the four countries of Polynesia in red and the eight territories in blue.

Page 39

A. **Marshall Islands:** Majuro
   Australia: Canberra
   Palau: Melekeok
   Kiribati: Tarawa
   Fiji: Suva
   Papua New Guinea: Port Moresby
   Vanuatu: Port Vila
   Samoa: Apia
   New Zealand: Wellington
   Tuvalu: Funafuti

B.

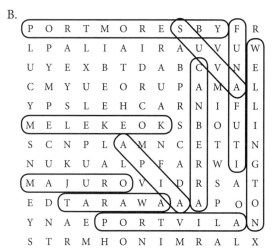

Page 40

Across
2. Micronesia
3. territory
6. Fiji
8. Queensland
10. Melbourne
12. Australia

Down
1. Victoria
4. Oceania
5. Polynesia
7. Melanesia
9. Nauru
11. Guam

Page 43

1. B   2. C   3. B   4. D   5. B

Page 44

A. 1. New Zealand
   2. Great Victoria Desert
   3. Mount Wilhelm
   4. Great Barrier Reef
   5. Mount Kosciuszko
   6. Simpson Desert
   7. New Zealand

Page 45

B. Students should color the mountains brown and Tasmania green. They should also circle the five deserts in yellow and the Great Barrier Reef in blue.

Page 47

A. 1. the Outback
   2. Great Victoria Desert
   3. Great Sandy Desert
   4. Gibson Desert
   5. Simpson Desert
   6. to keep cool during the hot days

B. Answers will vary—e.g., sand dunes, snakes, hopping mice, dry grasses, geckos, gravel hills

Page 48

A. Answers will vary—e.g., Yes, I would like to visit Ayers Rock to see the many caves where Aboriginal people made paintings and sculptures.

Page 49

B. 1. Northern
   2. Aboriginal
   3. sandstone
   4. caves
   5. Anungu
   6. Alice Springs

Crack the Code!

When it rains at Ayers Rock, the rock can appear <u>silver</u> in color.

Page 51

A. 1. sea turtles
2. kilometers
3. northeastern
4. algae
5. whale shark
6. birds
7. Pacific triton
8. polyps
9. millions
10. anemones

B. Answers will vary—e.g., Because algae covers most of the reef, it attracts many marine animals that eat it.

Page 53

1. volcanic
2. high
3. islet
4. lava
5. Vanuatu
6. Tuvalu
7. atoll
8. Tinakula
9. underwater eruptions

Page 54

Mountain	Height in Feet	Mountain Range	Country
Mt. Cook	12,316	Southern Alps	New Zealand
Mt. Kosciuszko	7,310	Great Dividing Range	Australia
Mt. Wilhelm	14,793	Bismarck Range	Papua New Guinea

Page 55

B.

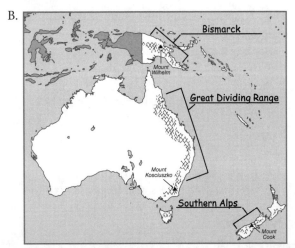

C. 1. e
2. g
3. c
4. h
5. a
6. d
7. b
8. f

Page 57

A. 1. Yes
2. No
3. No
4. No
5. Yes
6. Yes
7. No
8. No
9. Yes
10. No

B. 1. Temperate rainforests are located farther from the equator than tropical rainforests.
2. Temperate rainforests are found on the coast, whereas tropical rainforests can be found inland.
3. There are not as many different kinds of plants and animals in a temperate rainforest as in a tropical one.

Page 58

B. 1. Indian
2. Papua New Guinea
3. Tasman
4. Arafura
5. Cook
6. Torres
7. Great Australian Bight

C. a narrow channel of water that joins two larger bodies of water

Page 59

A.

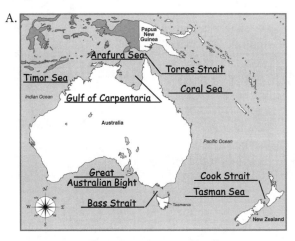

Page 60

A. 1. Milford Sound
2. about 20,000 years ago
3. a long and narrow inlet of sea that cuts into the land
4. They are shallower near the entrance to the sea.

Page 61

Answers will vary—e.g., The fjords of New Zealand are located on the southwest coast of South Island in a region called Fjordland.

Page 62

A. 1. No   4. No
   2. Yes   5. No
   3. Yes   6. Yes

Page 63

B.

Lake
Blue Lake
Frome Lake
Lake Barrine
Lake Disappointment
Lake Eyre
Lake Gairdner
Lake Mackay
Lake Torrens

C.
```
T H S Y F H O P E M A K R E W
O L E B B R C Y M E X L E U L
D I S A P P O I N T M E N T E
A W H R D O G M A L A O G A H
V E T R A E Q U E O C Y A R C
I O K I I H W O L A K D I E A
D A R N B O T U C E A I R L R
L I F E A L I K N O Y V D E W
E H R E T O R R E N S O N K N
D Y A D A Y T O S B L U E O T
E I M B T Y C U L H Y S R F E
```

Page 64

A.

Rank in Length	River
1	Murray River
2	Murrumbidgee River
3	Darling River
4	Lachlan River
5	Cooper Creek
6	Flinders River
7	Diamantina River

Page 65

B. Answers will vary—e.g., Many rivers in Australia are dry for part of the year. However, the Murray River in southeast Australia is a year-round river.

Page 66

Across	Down
1. Outback	2. Tasman
4. Wilhelm	3. temperate
6. sandstone	5. Murray
7. fjords	6. starfish

Page 69

1. C   2. D   3. A   4. B   5. A

Page 71

A. 1. Yes   6. No
   2. Yes   7. No
   3. No   8. No
   4. No   9. Yes
   5. Yes   10. No

B. 1. Victoria
   2. because they take millions of years to form
   3. Burning coal causes pollution, and mining for coal can do a lot of damage to the land.

Page 72

A. Manapouri, mountain, hall, penstocks, sea

Page 73

B. 1. turbines   4. reservoir
   2. electricity   5. Manapouri
   3. river   6. grates

Crack the Code!

The Manapouri turbines spin at a rate of 250 <u>revolutions</u> per minute.

Page 75

A. 1. f   2. c   3. e   4. g   5. a   6. h   7. d   8. b

B. Students should circle Australia, Fiji, and New Zealand in red.

```
W E F I J I N G R P L R I W
A L N Y T O I G A O S A U D
N A G O L D C O C L T D R N
E T N P A T K R H C L R A A
W E O A M D E L N E T S N X
Z M V L E A L O L R C M I N
E C H S E V R O R N A E U N
A R O I J I F E I D N O M P
L F L P E D P Z A M I A C E
A L U C P M I K E W L A U U
N Y C U L E B A U X I T E Q
D O A U S T R A L I A P E D
```

Page 77

A. 1. deserts
   2. Western Australia
   3. water
   4. Vineyards
   5. sugarcane
   6. Queensland
   7. Asia
   8. New South Wales

B. Pictures will vary—e.g., Students could draw and label a loaf of bread for wheat and a T-shirt for cotton.

Page 79

A. 1. stations
   2. Merino
   3. ringer
   4. sheepdog
   5. 77 million
   6. by people
   7. polyester
   8. 1,400
   9. 35%
   10. carpets

B. Answers will vary—e.g., If I was a Jillaroo on a sheep station, I would want to become the ringer of the sheep shed. I would really like working with the animals in the flock. But I would not like being so far away from town.

Page 81

A.

Rank	Country
1	Papua New Guinea
2	Kiribati
3	Federated States of Micronesia
4	Solomon Islands
5	Marshall Islands

B. 1. Palau
   2. Samoa
   3. 682,957 and 619,568
   4. Tuvalu and Vanuatu

C. Subsistence fishing is fishing done to feed yourself and your family. Commercial fishing is fishing done to catch huge amounts of fish to sell.

Page 83

1. Answers will vary—e.g., Oceanians make money as tour guides for people and by selling native crafts. Also, hotels and restaurants bring in money.
2. because it is easier to get to than many other South Pacific islands
3. to scuba dive and snorkel around the coral reef and see fish, caves, and even shipwrecks
4. Tourists who go to Samoa usually stay in fales and eat local food, shop at local markets, and take guided tours.
5. Answers will vary—e.g., I would go to Palau to see all the beautiful marine life—especially the millions of jellyfish in Jellyfish Lake.

Page 87

A. 1. gecko
   2. wallaby
   3. platypus
   4. kiwi
   5. Tasmanian devil
   6. Koalas
   7. platypus
   8. Kiwi
   9. Wallabies

B. Answers will vary—e.g., The platypus, because it is such an unusual mammal.

Page 88

Across
3. koalas
5. gold
6. Palau
7. kiwis

Down
1. coal
2. Manapouri
4. tuna
8. sheep

Page 91

1. C   2. C   3. D   4. A   5. B

Page 93

A. 1. Jorn Utzon
   2. royalty
   3. rooms
   4. coral reefs
   5. New Zealand
   6. carvings
   7. Pohnpei
   8. canoe
   9. unique
   10. treaty

B. Answers will vary—e.g., I would like to visit the Sydney Opera House because I've seen it in so many photos that I'd like to see it in person.

Page 95

A. 1. b   2. e   3. h   4. g   5. c   6. a   7. f   8. d
B. Students should color the picture and complete the caption.
   Captions will vary—e.g., Aboriginal art often features animals such as lizards.

Page 96

1. It brought 200 million dollars to the economy.
2. Producers used native music, decorations, and tribe names.
3. New Zealand has no squirrels.

Page 97

Answers will vary—e.g.,

First verse: A hobo sat under a tree beside a water hole. He sang while he waited for the water in his kettle to boil.

Second verse: When a sheep came to drink at the water hole, the hobo grabbed it and put it in his bag.

Third verse: The landowner and three policeman rode up on their horses and accused the hobo of taking the sheep.

Fourth verse: Rather than being caught, the hobo drowned himself in the water hole. Passersby can still hear his ghost singing.

Page 99

A. 1. No
   2. Yes
   3. No
   4. Yes
   5. No
   6. No
   7. Yes
   8. No
   9. Yes
   10. Yes
   11. Yes
   12. No

B. Answers will vary—e.g., I would try surfing because I love the water, and surfing sounds like a really fun sport.

Page 101

A. 1. Islam
   2. god
   3. Hinduism
   4. Christianity
   5. 17
   6. 1800s

B. Answers will vary—e.g.,
   1. They still honor their ancestors.
   2. because immigrants from Asia and the Middle East who move to Australia bring their religion with them

Page 103

1. because they moved frequently
2. the rules that govern Maori behavior and beliefs
3. a mythical time of creation according to the Aboriginal people
4. They help family members, even distant relatives, in times of need.
5. They traveled across the ocean in large canoes.
6. finding food and water
7. The payment makes up for the bride's family losing her company and help. It also shows that the groom's family values the bride.

Page 105

A.

Meat or Seafood	Vegetable or Fruit	Dessert	Other
emu	yam	Pavlova	damper
lobster	cassava	Lamingtons	Vegemite
wombat	breadfruit		
	papaya		
	taro root		

B. 1. Answers will vary—e.g., Pavlova, because I love fruit and whipped cream on dessert.
   2. Answers will vary—e.g., Crocodile, because I think it sounds gross!

Page 107

1. Kiribati
2. clay pots
3. formal
4. Sydney
5. canoes
6. January

Crack the Code!

The Motu made sails for their canoes using palm fronds, or leaves.

Page 108

Across	Down
3. voyage	1. football
4. Maori	2. carvings
7. breadfruit	5. Matilda
8. Islam	6. Dreamtime
10. Aborigines	9. surfing
11. Vegemite	

Page 110

1. Papua New Guinea
2. Great Sandy Desert
3. Great Dividing Range
4. Great Australian Bight
5. Murray River
6. Sydney
7. Pacific Ocean
8. Southern Alps
9. New Zealand
10. Fiji

Page 111

1. D   2. A   3. C   4. B   5. C   6. D   7. A   8. B

Page 112

9. B   10. A   11. C   12. B
13. B   14. C   15. D   16. A

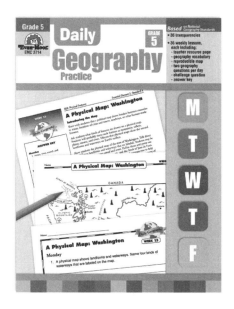

Daily Geography Practice

Based on the 18 National Geography Standards, *Daily Geography Practice* presents students with essential map-reading skills, geography terms, and more. Each book includes teacher resource pages, 36 transparencies, reproducible maps and activity pages, a glossary of geography terms, and answer keys. 160 pages *plus* 36 map transparencies.

Grade 1	EMC 3710-PRO
Grade 2	EMC 3711-PRO
Grade 3	EMC 3712-PRO
Grade 4	EMC 3713-PRO
Grade 5	EMC 3714-PRO
Grade 6+	EMC 3715-PRO

Fit standards-based geography practice into your curriculum!

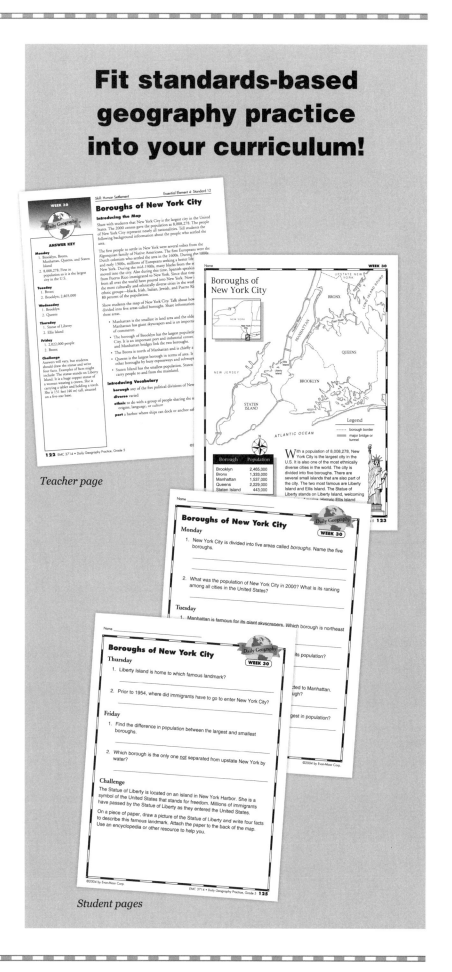

Teacher page

Student pages

Geography Centers

Hands-on support for your social studies curriculum! These centers provide a fun full-color format to practice geography literacy. Each book contains 12 or 13 self-contained centers aligned to the NCSS Standards. 192 full-color pages.
Federal Funding Sources I, V, 21.

Grades 1–2
Topics include positional words, following directions, keys and symbols, and landforms & waterways.

EMC 3716-PRO

Grades 2–3
Geography skills include globes and grids, locations of famous monuments, tourist maps, directions, and compass roses.

EMC 3717-PRO

Grades 3–4
Topics include parts of a map, continents and oceans, countries and regions in North America, and famous landmarks.

EMC 3718-PRO

Grades 4–5
Students learn tools of geography, including regions and time zones of the U.S., the 50 states, mystery countries, and globes and grids.

EMC 3719-PRO

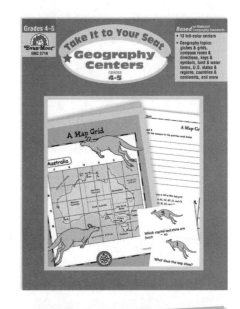

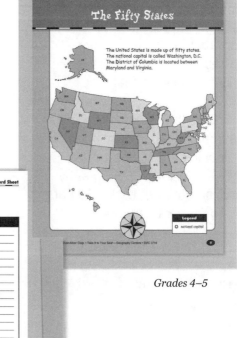

Grades 4–5

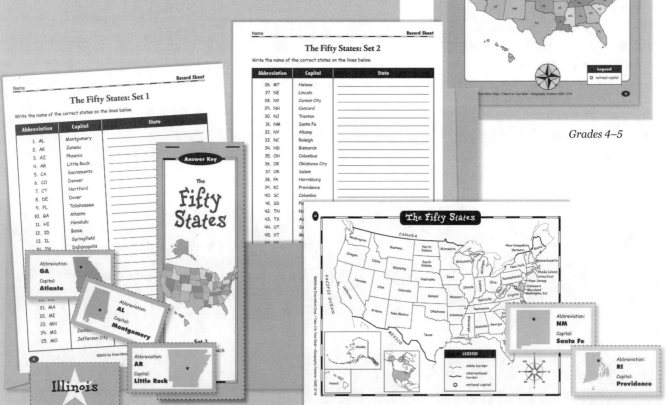